UNCONTROLLABLE
SPENDING
FOR
SOCIAL SERVICES
GRANTS

MARTHA DERTHICK

UNCONTROLLABLE SPENDING FOR SOCIAL SERVICES GRANTS

THE BROOKINGS INSTITUTION
WASHINGTON, D.C.

Library of Congress Cataloging in Publication Data:

Derthick, Martha.
    Uncontrollable spending for social services grants.
    Includes bibliographical references.
    1. Social service—United States—Finance.
2. Grants-in-aid—United States. I. Title.
HV95.D38   338.4′3   75-5155
ISBN 0-8157-1813-6

9 8 7 6 5 4

THE BROOKINGS INSTITUTION is an independent organization devoted to nonpartisan research, education, and publication in economics, government, foreign policy, and the social sciences generally. Its principal purposes are to aid in the development of sound public policies and to promote public understanding of issues of national importance.

The Institution was founded on December 8, 1927, to merge the activities of the Institute for Government Research, founded in 1916, the Institute of Economics, founded in 1922, and the Robert Brookings Graduate School of Economics and Government, founded in 1924.

The Board of Trustees is responsible for the general administration of the Institution, while the immediate direction of the policies, program, and staff is vested in the President, assisted by an advisory committee of the officers and staff. The by-laws of the Institution state: "It is the function of the Trustees to make possible the conduct of scientific research, and publication, under the most favorable conditions, and to safeguard the independence of the research staff in the pursuit of their studies and in the publication of the results of such studies. It is not a part of their function to determine, control, or influence the conduct of particular investigations or the conclusions reached."

The President bears final responsibility for the decision to publish a manuscript as a Brookings book. In reaching his judgment on the competence, accuracy, and objectivity of each study, the President is advised by the director of the appropriate research program and weighs the views of a panel of expert outside readers who report to him in confidence on the quality of the work. Publication of a work signifies that it is deemed a competent treatment worthy of public consideration but does not imply endorsement of conclusions or recommendations.

The Institution maintains its position of neutrality on issues of public policy in order to safeguard the intellectual freedom of the staff. Hence interpretations or conclusions in Brookings publications should be understood to be solely those of the authors and should not be attributed to the Institution, to its trustees, officers, or other staff members, or to the organizations that support its research.

Foreword

IN CLASSIFYING roughly three-fourths of the United States budget as "relatively uncontrollable" the President's budget office indicates that outlays for such items cannot be changed by government decisions except through a change in existing substantive law. By themselves, the President and his subordinates in the executive branch presumably cannot reduce "uncontrollable" budget items.

It is fair nevertheless to ask just how uncontrollable these so-called uncontrollables are and how they came to be that way. The executive branch has something to say about what goes into the nation's laws. It interprets the laws through regulations. It applies the regulations to particular cases; for example, an individual's application for social security benefits or a state or local government's application for grant-in-aid funds. At one or more of these points, it seems likely that the executive branch exercises discretion even in the administration of uncontrollable programs.

Without presuming that her conclusions would apply equally to other uncontrollable budget items, the author of this study scrutinizes executive actions with respect to a particular program—grants-in-aid to the states for social services. In this case, a drastic expansion of spending occurred during the first term of the Nixon administration, and this increase made social services grants a particularly interesting case for study. Why did this sudden outburst of spending occur, and how was it brought under control?

The search for the answers contributes much to an understanding of the inner workings of the Department of Health, Education, and Welfare, and of its relations with the President's budget office and with state governments. The author concludes that the law authorizing social services grants, while defective, did not deprive the executive branch of

vii

discretion. Rather, the law created a large and enticing opportunity for the states to exploit federal funds and made the executive branch bear virtually the whole burden of expenditure control. For a variety of reasons, which are discussed in detail, the executive branch proved unable—at least for a short time—to cope with that burden.

Martha Derthick is a senior fellow in the Governmental Studies program at Brookings. She wishes to thank Rosa Cook for the typing; colleagues Hugh Heclo and Richard P. Nathan and former colleague Gary Bombardier for comments on the manuscript; Gilbert Y. Steiner, the director of Governmental Studies, for comments and other aid; and Joy Silver for occasional research assistance. She is especially grateful to the many present and former public officials, both in the federal government and in Illinois, who granted interviews or commented on the manuscript.

The manuscript was edited by Tadd Fisher.

The Brookings Institution acknowledges a grant from the Edna McConnell Clark Foundation in partial support of this work. The foundation took no part in its direction, however, and the views expressed are solely those of the author and should not be attributed to the Clark Foundation or to the trustees, officers, or other staff members of the Brookings Institution.

KERMIT GORDON
President

March 1975
Washington, D.C.

Contents

CHAPTER ONE

The Social Services Loophole

IT IS A COMMONPLACE that the federal budget is out of control. The Office of Management and Budget (OMB) in the Executive Office of the President reported that 73.5 percent of the budget for fiscal year 1975 was "relatively uncontrollable," meaning that the terms of the government's obligation are fixed by law.[1] In 1974 when President Nixon announced the first budget ever to reach $300 billion, he said that 90 percent of the increase in spending over the preceding year was mandatory. He could not legally have avoided it.[2]

If most spending is determined by law, then controlling the level of spending is primarily a function of Congress, which enacts the laws. Moreover, when the President has tried to assert control over what is theoretically controllable by declining to spend appropriated funds, Congress and its partisans have counterattacked and proclaimed the legislature's constitutional right to say how much money shall be spent and for what purposes. Congress was challenged by President Nixon's use of impoundments and by his charge that it acts irresponsibly. Hence, efforts at reforming budget processes in recent years have focused on Congress, which has sought to meet the executive's challenge.[3]

In view of the executive's control over program planning, administration, and budget preparation, however, it is also fair to ask how well the executive branch performs. While the President and the members of the Executive Office have been proclaiming their own lack of power and pointing at Congress, how responsibly have they themselves acted? In practice, responsibility for spending is shared by the branches, and if spending is out of control, responsibility for that is shared too.

This study, an inquiry into executive control of spending, examines a program in which control was conspicuously lacking for several years: grants-in-aid to the states for social services under the public assistance titles of the Social Security Act. As a welfare program, social services grants are one among a large, varied, and ever-growing array of efforts by the federal government to help the poor, the sick, and the handicapped. The Department of Health, Education, and Welfare (HEW), with more than 120,000 employees and a budget of over $100 billion, administers most of these efforts. As grants-in-aid, services expenditures likewise are part of a large ($50 billion a year) and increasing (at a rate of nearly 20 percent a year) supply of federal assistance to state and local governments. Especially in the fields of health, education, and welfare, the federal government carries out many of its domestic purposes by giving grants to governments at lower levels of the federal system. Spending for social services grants soared from $354 million in fiscal year 1969 to $1.69 billion in fiscal year 1972. Other welfare programs and other grants-in-aid were rising too; grants to the states for Aid to Families with Dependent Children—a big program of cash assistance to the poor—doubled between 1969 and 1972, as did grants for Medicaid, which pays the medical expenses of the poor. Social services grants, however, by more than quadrupling far exceeded the pace of even these two.

Exactly what federal services grants were spent for, no one knows; the inability of governments to account in detail for the spending is part of this story. A private accounting firm's study in 1972 found that 25 percent went for child foster care and 15 percent for child care, presumably in day nurseries.[4] The rest was widely distributed among myriad activities such as special services for handicapped children, homemaker and chore services, employment and training, treating alcoholism and drug addiction, and providing care to the mentally ill and retarded. The same study also showed that, in general, the huge increase in federal expenditures did not increase the volume of such activities. State governments substituted the federal funds for their own funds. Had the federal government exercised more control, presumably the money would have been spent more effectively. It might have been used to expand social services, or federal policymakers might have chosen a different use of the money altogether, such as increasing the cash incomes of the poor.

In the technical language of OMB, social services grants were "uncontrollable" because "open-ended." The law did not put a ceiling on the amount that could be spent, but rather obligated the federal government to match whatever state governments spent for a particular activity—that is, for "social services." How much the federal government spent therefore depended on what the states claimed and what HEW allowed. Congress finally did close the open end on social services spending with a $2.5 billion ceiling enacted late in 1972, but only after social services had turned into one of the biggest federal grant-in-aid programs.

The nearly $1.7 billion expended as social services grants in 1972 was no trivial sum, even by the standards of the time. It exceeded, for example, the construction outlays of the Corps of Engineers, spending for urban renewal by the Department of Housing and Urban Development, and spending on manned space flights by the National Aeronautics and Space Administration. It was sizable also in comparison with other welfare programs, such as food stamps, an important type of income subsidy, which cost the federal government $1.9 billion, or even Aid to Families with Dependent Children, for which the federal government spent $3.6 billion.

Still, what made this program remarkable was neither its size nor its exceptionally rapid rate of growth, but the fact that neither was intended by the legislature or the chief executive. The President's budget estimate of $937 million for services grants in 1972 was too low by nearly a billion dollars. The Senate Finance Committee, after reviewing the legislative history, concluded in 1972 that "the use of 75 percent Federal matching for 'social services' [has broadened] far beyond anything intended by the Congress."[5] On the floor of the House of Representatives, Chairman Wilbur Mills of the Ways and Means Committee denounced social services as "the worst loophole that has ever been written into the law on the financing of Government."[6]

To say that neither the President nor Congress planned this expenditure is of course not the same as saying that no one in the federal government planned it. For some years administrators of federal welfare programs, who were professionals in the field of social work, had looked forward to a time when federal funds would help state and local governments finance a comprehensive and varied range of social services. Such services were to begin, but certainly not end, with the very poor who were on welfare. A report of the Advisory Council on Public Welfare to the secretary of health, education, and welfare may be taken as a definitive statement of this official view. It recommended that "social services through public welfare programs be strengthened and extended and be readily accessible as a matter of right at all times to all who need them."[7] It was the professionals' pursuit of this goal that initially accounted for the federal government's decision to give social services grants: the professionals inspired the law. Yet they did not foresee or intend the outcome of 1972, when social services grants became a form of "back-door revenue sharing," as the *Washington Post* put it, through which federal funds poured for purposes that no one in Washington knew and for which the states could offer no accounting. This was not the fulfillment of the professionals' ideal—it was a travesty. They had wanted the painstaking cultivation of professional specialties under Washington's guidance. As it turned out, guidance floundered in a gusher of federal funds.

Some welfare professionals, watching the transformation of social services grants into a measure of fiscal relief for the states, suspected the Nixon administration of contriving as much. In January 1971 the President proclaimed the New American Revolution, from which state and local governments would gain new power and vitality through federal revenue sharing. The explosion of social services spending followed shortly. Perhaps the Nixon administration, doubting the political feasibility of its revenue-sharing proposals, pursued its purposes indirectly by permitting the states to exploit social services grants. But this is implausible. There is no reason to presume stealth as a Nixon strategy for reforming the federal system and much reason to doubt that services grants suited the administration's reform purposes. Unlike the Nixon proposals for special revenue sharing, services grants did not replace a series of categorical grants. They were new money. Nor were they allocated rationally by a statutory formula designed to discourage grantsmanship, the rival enterprise of state governments for a share. On the contrary, social services represented grantsmanship gone wild. A few states began as big winners, and competition among them, in the absence of a spending limit, threatened an unending spiral. And if services grants were unsuitable as special revenue sharing, they were unnecessary as, and ultimately a threat to, general revenue sharing, the administration's proposal for giving the states a fresh supply of unrestricted funds. General revenue sharing passed in the fall of 1972, but only after Congress closed the open end on services grants. The Senate Finance Committee in particular was unwilling to enact general revenue sharing as long as services funds flowed freely. The administration pursued the planned initiative for which it could take public credit—general revenue sharing.

It is ironic that the "worst loophole" enlarged greatly under a Republican administration that was managerial in style and committed by the campaign rhetoric of its leader to the proposition that *every* federal activity is—and must be—a candidate for expenditure control."[8] True, the Nixon White House of 1969 advanced a costly proposal for welfare reform, the Family Assistance Plan (FAP); but this only deepens the irony, for with the FAP the administration explicitly embraced an "income" rather than a "services" strategy for helping the poor.[9] When free to choose in 1969, the President chose the FAP, yet his administration's legacy to national welfare programs as of 1975 is not the planned reform, which would have increased the cash incomes of poor individuals, but the large unplanned expansion of grants to the states for social services.*

How, then, did this "accident" occur? The Office of Management and Budget in the Executive Office of the President has procedures to protect the President against this sort of surprise and to safeguard a range of budgetary choice for him. Where did the procedures fail? And what of general import can be learned from the failure?

As the following account will show, the President's budget staff did not play a very large part either in initiating federal grants for social services or, what is more surprising, in bringing them under control. Most executive action took place within the administering department, HEW. There, responsibility was diffuse and shifted often as a result of reorganizations and the normal changes of leadership that follow a change in party control of the presidency. In theory, of course, no matter how the features of departmental organization may change, major decisions are made by appointive officials—the secretary, under secretary, assistant secretaries, and others lower down who hold appointive positions as heads of units with responsibility for particular aspects of the department's activity.† These are the officials—partisans, ordinarily—who owe their jobs directly or indirectly to the President and who make

---

* Other important legacies are a tenfold increase in federal expenditures for food stamps; a national minimum income for the aged, blind, and disabled; and an automatic adjustment of social security benefits to increases in the cost of living.

† See appendix A for a chart of the organization of HEW in 1971.

policy on his behalf. Again in theory, the bureaucracy of career civil servants takes policy guidance from them. Thus, the executive branch responds to the preferences of its elected head, the President; but recent presidents have often complained that it does not respond very well. Social services grants may seem to be a case in point. For social services spending to explode during a Republican administration is baffling unless the bureaucracy sabotaged the administration's intent.

Such an explanation of what happened would fit much current theory about the power of professional bureaucracies, but it does not happen to fit the facts of the case.

CHAPTER TWO

A Loose Law

OFFICIALLY, the Department of Health, Education, and Welfare (HEW) blamed the law for the loophole. "Under the law . . . the sky's the limit," Under Secretary John G. Veneman told a congressional committee in 1972.[1] By defining services and beneficiaries broadly and by mandating federal matching of state expenditures, the law created an infinite federal obligation, HEW argued. Valid to a degree, this explanation nonetheless fails to account satisfactorily for the timing of the explosion in expenditures, which occurred in 1972. For a decade before then, expenditures had grown slowly, as table 1 shows. Yet the essential elements of the law were in place as of 1962. Insofar as the loophole was in the law, it was largely created then.

The Public Welfare Amendments of 1962, sponsored by the Kennedy administration, initiated a more or less distinct category of grants to the states for social services. This category became an adjunct to the several categories of grants for cash support and medical service to the poor—Old Age Assistance, Aid to the Blind, Aid to the Permanently and Totally Disabled, Aid to Families with Dependent Children, Medical Assistance to the Aged, and after 1965, "Medicaid"—which together constituted the federal public assistance program. Matching funds had been available before for service-giving within the public assistance program, but incidentally and without much encouragement to the states to perform. As Abraham Ribicoff, secretary of health, education, and welfare, explained to President Kennedy, the department sought in 1962 to reorient "the whole approach to welfare from a straight cash handout operation to one in which the emphasis is on rehabilitation of those on relief and prevention ahead of time." Ribicoff promised the President that in this way both liberals and conservatives could "be allied to the cause of welfare revision."[2] The new law required the states to provide

TABLE 1. *Federal Grants to the States for Social
Services, 1963–1972*

Fiscal year	Grants[a] (thousands of dollars)
1963	194,304
1964	244,437
1965	295,142
1966	359,165
1967	281,589
1968	346,654
1969	354,491
1970	522,005
1971	740,958
1972	1,688,432

Sources: For fiscal years 1963–70: *Departments of Labor and Health, Education, and Welfare Appropriations for 1973*, Hearings before a Subcommittee of the House Committee on Appropriations, 92 Cong. 2 sess. (1972), pt. 5, p. 239. For fiscal years 1971–72: "State Expenditures for Public Assistance Programs Approved under Titles I, IV-A, X, XIV, XVI, and XIX of the Social Security Act," issued annually by the Department of Health, Education, and Welfare, Social and Rehabilitation Service, Office of Financial Management.

a. Through fiscal year 1966, social services grants were combined with grants for administration and training. They did not become a separate budget item until 1967.

services to welfare recipients and authorized federal payment of 75 percent of the cost, which was then a very high rate compared with that of most federal grant programs or the previous matching rate (50 percent) of administrative costs in the public assistance program. Several elements of the law later turned out to be very important: it failed to define services clearly, authorized state public assistance agencies to purchase services from other state agencies, and authorized federal funds for the cost of services given to former and potential as well as present recipients of welfare.[3]

The law did not define services; it merely stated their purpose. At various points it referred to self-support, self-care, strengthening family life, and preventing and reducing dependency as the goals of services. HEW's legislative draftsman, Assistant General Counsel Sidney Saperstein, foresaw that the lack of definition would raise problems of interpretation. It would be hard to distinguish between services and other kinds of administrative activity. And, he asked, just what services would qualify for the 75 percent matching rate? Medical care services, for example? Saperstein observed that such questions might prove troublesome in view of the high matching rate and the lack of an expenditure ceiling. He made a note to himself to raise these questions with Wilbur Cohen, HEW's assistant secretary for legislation and the principal author of the bill, from whom Saperstein was getting instructions. Years later neither could remember precisely what Cohen had answered, but during an interview Cohen was quick to acknowledge an impatience with the niceties of legal definition. "Sid—Sid's a friend of mine—Sid would always say, 'I've got these 372 problems. . . .' I'd say, 'Put it in regulations . . . do it later. I can't think of an answer.'" Cohen was prepared to let definitions emerge from experience.

In 1962 the decision was indeed to leave the question of definition to regulations. The law provided that the federal government would match 75 percent of the cost of services "prescribed" or "specified" by the secretary of HEW, the prescribed services to be required of the states if they were to qualify for the new matching funds, the specified services to be optional.* Apart from a lawyer's anxieties, there appears to have been no disposition in HEW to write more of a definition into the law. Welfare professionals in the Bureau of Family Services (BFS) knew more or less what they meant by "services." Fundamentally and at a minimum, it meant casework by a trained social worker. Beyond that it could mean such traditional things as providing homemakers for invalid adults or finding foster homes for neglected children. Ultimately it could mean anything that would help troubled, handicapped, and dependent people. To attempt precise legal definitions in 1962 would have been difficult conceptually and also bureaucratically, for it would have stirred conflicts within HEW between the BFS and other units, especially the Children's Bureau and the Office of Vocational Rehabilitation (OVR), which also had services functions. It followed that the definition of services should be developed administratively.

Whereas jurisdictional tensions within HEW helped render the law mute in the matter of definition, they fostered language authorizing the

---

* In practice, the distinction between "prescribed" and "specified" services was unclear because definitions of services were generally unclear. The Bureau of Family Services' guidance to the states defined services in terms of purpose or of social problems rather than in terms of method. The BFS conceived of prescribed services as the minimum necessary to help persons in greatest need, wheras specified services were to extend "beyond the minimum and . . . give emphasis to services for preventive purposes." (Sec. 4640, pt. 4, "Handbook of Public Assistance Administration," transmitted by BFS State Letter 606 [November 30, 1962; processed].)

purchase of services, the second major element of the legal loophole. The law authorized federal matching for services purchased from state health agencies, or vocational rehabilitation agencies, "or any other State agency which the Secretary may determine to be appropriate."[4] This passage and a preceding one that prohibited public assistance funds from being used for vocational rehabilitation services were designed to prevent the BFS from invading the jurisdiction of the OVR. No part of the law in 1962 was more subject to negotiations and redrafting, for vocational rehabilitation agencies insisted on the firmest protection. The administration's draft bill originally provided that state public assistance agencies might purchase services from private agencies, but vocational rehabilitation agencies objected to this, again fearing displacement.[5] The final version provided only for indirect purchase from private sources; that is, the state public assistance agency might purchase from other state agencies, which could supply services either through their own staffs or through contracts with private or local public sources.

Just how to word the purchase provision was considered with some care because the BFS recognized that purchase was open to exploitation. Director Kathryn Goodwin noted in a memorandum the bureau's "concern about costs because of likely pressure on the part of voluntary and some public agencies to sell services."[6] Accordingly, both the statute and the congressional committee reports on the bill incorporated safeguards drafted by the BFS. The statute provided that purchased services would be "subject to limitations prescribed by the Secretary." The House Ways and Means Committee believed that "in most instances the normal range of services provided by the public welfare department will be sufficient to meet the normal needs. When this method of providing services [purchase] is used, your committee anticipates that the services to be purchased will be reimbursed on a case-by-case basis, and not by a lump-sum payment." The Senate Finance Committee said it did not "anticipate that the public welfare programs will be used to finance the cost of services normally the responsibility of another State agency."[7] The provisions about purchase, like the lack of definitions, made Saperstein nervous. He feared leaving too much to the secretary's discretion and thereby increasing "the extent of the pressure which may be exerted on the Secretary."[8] Congress approved the purchase provisions, Congressman Wilbur Mills later said, "blinded and failing to understand."[9]

HEW officials prepared the section covering former and potential recipients without any apparent fear that it would permit spending to get out of control, although to later critics of the department, offering services coverage so broadly seemed obviously to invite abuse. "All of us" are potential receivers, Congresswoman Martha W. Griffiths of Michigan pointed out to Under Secretary Veneman in 1972, challenging him to deny it. "Under a potential receiver you can pick up Christina Ford and John D. Rockefeller."[10] Actually, the law did not use the term "potential" but referred to persons who were "likely to become" applicants or recipients of aid.[11] BFS guidance to the states in 1962 defined potential applicants and recipients as "those families and adults whose economic, personal or social situation, separately or in combination, would reasonably be expected to result in need for financial assistance under one of the public assistance titles within one year after the request."[12] In 1962, however, officials of the BFS believed it would be some years before state public assistance agencies would have enough trained caseworkers or funds to extend services beyond the population of recipients. In answer to questions from Senator Harry Byrd of Virginia, Secretary Ribicoff assured the Finance Committee that services would not be extended broadly.[13] BFS officials, while privately viewing broad extension as desirable, quite honestly saw it as something that would happen over the long run.

These features of the law—the lack of definitions, the authorization of purchase from other state agencies, and the authorization of services for former and potential recipients—eventually fed on one another to create a large opportunity for exploitation, but this could not have happened had the law not been open-ended. In that respect, services grants conformed to the pattern of the parent law, and, because they conformed, no one in Congress or the executive branch seems to have given much thought in 1962 to the implications. The authorization of grants for services was grafted onto the public assistance titles of the Social Security Act, which since 1935 had authorized federal financial participation in the states' support of the dependent poor. The public assistance titles had always been open-ended; that is, Congress had obligated the federal government to match what the states spent no matter how many recipients there turned out to be. Because the number of recipients and the size of state expenditures could fluctuate with economic conditions and with the states' own decisions about eligibility and levels of payment, it was impractical for Congress to fix a level of expenditures in advance. Nevertheless, Congress did limit the federal obligation somewhat by putting a ceiling on the amount the federal government would spend per recipient. Federal grants for services, coming after a generation's experience of grants for money payments, were like the grants for money payments in that Congress set no overall spending ceiling but unlike them in that there was not even a limit per recipient. Besides, the former-and-potential language meant that expenditures were not limited to present recipients. Under the law, then, federal grants for services were even less controllable and less predictable than were grants for cash payments to the poor.

In the early 1970s, after the loophole had been found and HEW had to account to Congress for what happened, the department usually identified 1967 as the year in which the story should start. This made the timing of the spending explosion less of a puzzle; the explosion appeared to follow Social Security Act amendments made at that time. Changes did enlarge the loophole then but were nowhere near as important as subsequent statements by administrators made them seem. The amendments of 1967 required the states to furnish child-care services and to offer family planning services to people who were referred to the secretary of labor for work training under the act; thus two categories of service were mandated, with the objectives of increasing employment, reducing illegitimate births, and "otherwise strengthening family life." The purchase of service from private sources was authorized "to the extent specified by the Secretary." Certain changes in definitional language were made. Whereas the law of 1962 had omitted any definition, scattered fragments of purposive language were now brought together in a formal, if circular, definition of family services: "services to a family or any member thereof for the purpose of preserving, rehabilitating, reuniting, or strengthening the family, and such other services as will assist members of a family to attain or retain capability for the maximum self-support and personal independence."[14] This was what the federal government promised to share the costs of, and it was still so vague that the department would have to clarify it in regulations. The secretary's authority to do this, however, was weakened by another change in the law. The language of 1962 had authorized matching funds for services specified or prescribed by the secretary. This made plain that, for purposes of federal matching, services were what the secretary of HEW said they were. The omission of these phrases in 1967 deprived the secretary of a firm statutory defense when states started making claims for activities they called services. The burden of proof that the claims were invalid now fell on HEW. Still, this breach was confined to one category of public assistance, Aid to Families with Dependent Children (AFDC). The so-called adult titles of the act, covering aid to the aged, the aged who were medically indigent, the blind, and the disabled, retained the old "specified" and "prescribed" language.

HEW officials argued in 1972 that the crucial characteristic of the law was that it left them no discretion; they had to spend whatever the states claimed. The truth is that it gave them virtually unlimited discretion, without much in the way of protection when pressures developed. The vagueness of the law had created a vast area of administrative choice. It was simply not clear what was authorized to be done, on behalf of whom, or by what state agencies.

Inherent in the concept of social services, which encompass a wide variety of activity, vagueness resulted also from conflicting intentions underlying the law. As Secretary Ribicoff had said to the President, the services approach was appealing because it united conservatives and liberals, the former believing that services would reduce dependency, the latter believing that they would succor the poor; the former believing that money would be saved, the latter believing it would be spent to good purpose. Ambiguity was the great advantage of social services as public policy and broadened the scope and heightened the importance of administrative discretion even when congressional statements about services were relatively precise.

The conflict of purposes was never sharper than in 1967, which helps to explain subsequent administrative action and congressional reaction with regard to services. President Johnson's proposals, originating in HEW and supported generally by welfare professionals and allied liberals, sought as usual to extend benefits for the poor. Congress, on the other hand, faced with a sharp rise in dependency and in public resentment of it, was determined to cut back on welfare programs, reduce illegitimate births, and get recipients to go to work. A law was drafted through "the dynamic of the two Wilburs," as one observer put it— Mills for the legislative branch and Cohen for the executive—pragmatists both, impelled toward accommodation by a shared understanding that it is vital to the writing of laws on difficult questions in a vast democracy. In 1967 this dynamic was dominant; the law evolved during three months of almost daily executive sessions in which Mills with the Ways and Means membership and Cohen for HEW conducted negotiations. "Every time the committee said 'work,' " an HEW source later recalled, "Wilbur said 'day care.' "

In the end Congress required the states to refer all "appropriate" recipients of AFDC to work-training programs and required the Department of Labor to set up such programs wherever a large number of recipients lived. Simultaneously, it acknowledged the necessity for a much larger expenditure for day care, which a Senate Finance Committee report said would "be needed in great volume under the bill." The same report also introduced the concept of eligibility for whole groups of the population; it said that services to help families remain independent might be made available to "those who need them in low-income neighborhoods and . . . other groups that might otherwise include more AFDC cases."[15] Here was fairly clear language, no less valid as an expression of legislative intent for having been turned by administrative hands. Yet it veiled very different purposes. Whereas Congress meant to encourage the welfare poor to go to work, Wilbur Cohen had taken another step toward the long-range goal of broad provision of social services. That was the significance of group eligibility, which departed from the announced intentions of 1962. If giving services did not depend on determinations of individual eligibility, the possibilities for providing service increased enormously. Group eligibility, an HEW official said simply, was "dynamite." This was another element in the making of the loophole.

In summary, the law gave great discretion to administrators, and administrators of public assistance in HEW were inclined to promote the extension of services. This begins to explain what happened but still fails to answer why federal services grants grew so suddenly and with so little administrative supervision in the early 1970s.

CHAPTER THREE

Administrative Reorganization

THE ADMINISTRATION of services grants changed fundamentally in the late 1960s. Begun as an adjunct to the public assistance program, services grants had been administered by the Bureau of Family Services (BFS), which had been founded in 1936 as the Bureau of Public Assistance (BPA) and renamed in 1962 in acknowledgment of the new emphasis.* In 1967, a reorganization changed this. Responsibility for services was lodged collectively in a new organization, the Social and Rehabilitation Service (SRS), but within SRS it was scattered among several subunits that each specialized in a different component of the population. In the short run this produced chaos. More to the point, it produced a thoroughly different conception of how services grants should be spent and supervised. Regulations that governed the program in its explosive phase were prepared by the new regime and were issued in January 1969, just before the Nixon administration took office.[1]

In substance, the reorganization of 1967 renewed the emphasis on rehabilitation and services in the public assistance program. The first administrator of SRS, Mary Switzer, was favorably regarded in Congress for the well-publicized successes of the Vocational Rehabilitation Administration (formerly the Office of Vocational Rehabilitation), which she had headed for seventeen years. "A dynamo," John W. Gardner, secretary of health, education, and welfare, said of her in announcing the choice.[2] Leaders of the Department of Health, Education, and Welfare (HEW) thought that if anyone could help the welfare poor get to work and show Congress that HEW was trying, Mary Switzer could. The reorganization coincided with consideration of the Social Security Act amendments of 1967 and may have been meant to increase congres-

---

* The contrived compound BPA/FS is occasionally used hereafter to denote the historical bureau of 1935–67.

15

sional confidence in the department's administration of welfare programs at that critical time.[3]

Organizationally, SRS increased generalist, centralized control of hitherto separate specialized agencies, some of which had reported directly to the HEW secretary. It brought together in one component of HEW the Vocational Rehabilitation Administration, the Administration on Aging, the Mental Retardation Division of the Bureau of Health Services in the Public Health Service, and the Welfare Administration, which consisted of the Bureau of Family Services and the Children's Bureau, and made them responsible to an appointive official, the SRS administrator, who in turn would report to the secretary. An administrator's office began to develop with responsibility for such functions as program planning, evaluation, research, and statistics, with staff drawn from the subunits.

The proliferation of narrow professional specialties in HEW had followed from the post–New Deal proliferation of government functions, within the framework of a public service traditionally specialized. In HEW and other federal departments, bureaus have typically been staffed by specialists in the particular function the organization performs, and those who perform the specialty in varying degrees have developed the characteristics of a profession, with some presumption to esoteric knowledge or skills and with particularized, self-enforced standards of admission. The proliferation of specialties and the apparent growth in the power of professional bureaucracies have raised in acute form the issue of how coordination and control are to be imposed. It is an issue that much troubles the modern welfare state. The response has been to balance the professional specialists with generalists. This can be done in three ways: by changing the composition of the bureaucracy through an admixture of civil servants *not* specialized by profession (they may think of themselves simply as "public administrators"); by giving the leading generalists—elected chief executives or department heads—larger staffs with broader functions and encouraging such staffs to supervise specialists more aggressively; or by adding new layers of generalist supervision over specialized operating units. The creation of SRS was an example of the last of these techniques.

With the characteristic perspective of the central coordinator, Secretary Gardner promised that the new "unified" approach to the problems of individuals and families would be better than the old "fragmented" approach. In itself, the new organization was not a very large step toward generalist control. Several of the old units were incorporated more or less intact: the Vocational Rehabilitation Administration became the Rehabilitation Services Administration (RSA), the Children's Bureau remained the Children's Bureau, and the Administration on Aging stayed the same. A veteran program specialist headed the lot. Nevertheless, it was a first step toward generalist direction, and it was duplicated in the regions. SRS regional commissioners were named and given authority to supervise all SRS programs and activities in their regions and to approve all state plans. This was meant to interrupt ties between program specialists in the field and in Washington. In most of the regional offices, as in Washington, the new chief executive was drawn from the Vocational Rehabilitation Administration.

With regard to services, the reorganization affected two of the old subunits more than the rest—the Bureau of Family Services, which lost control of services spending, and the Children's Bureau, which gained great responsibility but at the cost of severe internal stress.

The BFS had had responsibility both for grants to the states for cash payments to the poor and for services grants under the public assistance titles. One purpose of the reorganization was to separate administration of the two kinds of grants as a first step toward separation at the state and local levels. Thus, within SRS, responsibility for cash support of the poor was now lodged in the Assistance Payments Administration (APA). Most of the BFS personnel went there. If the BFS had a lineal successor in the SRS, it was APA. Personnel of the Division of Welfare Services in the BFS, not a large number in any case, were divided among other units in SRS—the Children's Bureau, the Administration on Aging, a new Medical Services Administration, and the RSA. Much of the BFS went on more or less as before, but the part that had been responsible for services disintegrated—"scattered to the winds," said one who experienced the change. The reorganization, abruptly announced, was very hard on morale.

The Children's Bureau seemingly stood to benefit from the rising interest in day-care centers and the growing availability of federal funds for helping poor children. It now was in charge of providing services to children on Aid to Families with Dependent Children, a responsibility that it would have welcomed in 1935 but that it did not consider an unalloyed blessing some thirty years later. The bureau was a small, elite organization of veteran professionals who gave technical assistance to the states and set standards of professional leadership. They distributed more knowledge than money. Their grant programs were minuscule compared with public assistance. They had concentrated on rural areas and worked through county and state governments. To undertake the mass provision of services to a huge dependent population in urban settings would require a thorough change in the bureau's philosophy and mode of operations. In 1968, a new associate director arrived at the bureau who sought to manage this change. He was Jule Sugarman, a career civil servant, who was brought to HEW in one of a series of moves by the department's leadership to secure control over Head Start, the highly popular child-care program of the Office of Economic Opportunity (OEO), of which he had been associate director. Sugarman had held a number of executive positions in the federal government, but his career was unusual in that it covered many agencies. He was a generalist in a career service where specialization is the norm. He had worked successively in the Civil Service Commission, Bureau of the Budget, Bureau of Prisons, and Bureau of Inter-American Affairs of the Department of State before going to OEO. His proposals to Mary Switzer for the Children's Bureau called for a massive shake-up and great stress on generalist control.[4] In child welfare, a field where professionals have been dominant, this was his undoing. He did not become bureau chief or director of the newly created Office of Child Development in the Office of the Secretary, but before leaving HEW in 1970 he had considerable influence on the course that services spending took. With Switzer, he prevailed in the preparation of the regulations of 1969.

The new regime was strongly expansionist with regard to social services. It wanted the states to do much more. This attitude, however, did not distinguish it from the old regime. The head of the Welfare Administration between 1962 and 1967, Ellen Winston, had been named to the job because of her record in establishing service programs in North Carolina. Under her leadership the BFS constantly exhorted the states to greater effort; services were gospel after 1962. The crucial difference was that under the old regime expansion had been contained by a narrow conception of services and by certain deeply held doctrines of public administration.

Historically, the BFA/FS had been staffed by professional social workers who conceived of services as casework by a trained person. The worker should assist the client in making use of organized sources of help, but the essence of service was the interaction of the worker with the person in need of help. BFS rules for services grants were based on this assumption. Designed to promote casework, these rules required state public assistance agencies to classify cases according to the volume of services needed, and they set standards for caseloads, the ratio of supervisors to workers, the frequency of home visits, and the training of workers. Given this conception, federal grants went mainly to pay a share of the salaries of workers in the public assistance program. When the BFS lost control of services, a change began to occur, indicated at first less by what regulations said than by what they failed to say. In 1969 all the old requirements covering caseloads and college degrees for workers and the like were dropped, over the strenuous objections of the one survivor from the BFS who participated in preparing the regulations. In official language, a distinction soon began to develop between "soft" and "hard" services. Advice and counseling from a caseworker were "soft" in this managerial parlance and presumably less valuable than day-care centers, or drug treatment programs, or work training, which were "hard" and which were much more widely available in 1969 than in 1962 because of the intervening growth of public programs for social purposes. The changed conception and changed social context helped lay the basis for granting funds for a much wider range of activity than the daily routines of caseworkers.[5]

A change in policy toward the purchase of services was crucial to effectuating the changed conception. The law had been broadened in 1967 to permit purchase from private sources, and that was important; but more important was the reversal of administrative attitudes. The BFS had been cautious about purchase and determined to use it sparingly. The new regime made a wholesale commitment.

The BFS staff foresaw that purchase, in combination with the open end, could be exploited by the states, which might be tempted to apply federal public assistance funds to the cost of schools, hospitals, or other activities generally available to the public. The BFS feared this both because its own goal of increased service to the poor would be sacrificed and because abuse could jeopardize the open end. Congress might crack down. Caution therefore pervaded the bureau's policies on purchase. State public assistance agencies were instructed that purchase should not be used to pay for activities that normally were the responsibility of other state agencies and should not replace "present levels of effort by other state agencies in respect to public assistance clients." Purchase was supposed to expand services by increasing either the number of clients served or the kinds of service and was limited to health departments, education departments, vocational rehabilitation agencies, and employment services.[6] Payment had to be on an individual case basis.

In its actual supervision of purchase arrangements, the bureau was similarly cautious. The only test of its policy came in California, which alone among the states sought to use purchase in a substantial way. In 1966 the California Department of Social Welfare contracted with the Department of Education for a preschool compensatory program for children from low-income families. Officials from the BFS headquarters went to California to review the proposed program personally; attached three pages of detailed conditions before approving the interdepartmental agreement, mostly for the purpose of controlling costs; and specified that approval was for a year only, on an experimental basis. After six months the agency was to make a report, and after a year federal officials would conduct their own review.[7]

The Vocational Rehabilitation Administration had relied heavily and successfully on purchase, a technique that increased flexibility, controlled staff size, and created a network of organizational allies, who were dependents of the purchasing organizations. Having tested purchase in one program and found it satisfactory, Mary Switzer proceeded to extend it to the public assistance program. In this she was joined by Jule Sugarman, whose plans for day-care centers depended on purchase. In 1969, nearly all the restrictive language on purchase was dropped, including the requirement for states to increase their efforts on behalf of the poor. Exhortation superseded caution. The new rules positively required states to increase their use of purchase. State plans were to "assure progressive development of arrangements with a number and variety of agencies . . . with the aim of providing opportunities for individuals to exercise choice with regard to the source of purchased service."[8]

Underlying these changes in regulations were sharply different beliefs about relations with the states and even about the conduct of public administration generally. The BPA/FS was thoroughly regulatory and hortatory. Having a clear doctrine of what public assistance administration ought to be like, it set high standards of conduct for the states, spelled them out at great length in "state letters," and worked with utmost determination for some thirty years to bring state governments up to the standards.[9] States were held strictly responsible for meeting the federal requirements, and the key to securing responsibility, according to bureau doctrine, was the presence in each state of a single agency answerable to the bureau in Washington for execution of the state program. (Hence the great importance of the single-state-agency requirement, which the regulations of 1969 did not revise but which crumbled later under accumulated pressure for services spending.) There was a distinct moralism in the approach. One person who had served in a state public assistance agency and moved to the BPA in the 1950s reflected on this quality in an interview: "Before I came to the BPA, I always wondered which the 'good' states were. When I arrived in Washington I learned there were no good states. There were states that had some good things about them, but there were no *good* states."

The explanations for the bureau's highly regulatory mode are to be found partly in the nature of the program, which has involved very large sums of money and considerable potential for corruption and controversy, and partly in the nature of a guiding personality, Jane Hoey, who was chief from 1936 to 1953. Hoey was the founder and dominating spirit of what I have called the "old regime," and its decline began with her departure. The reorganization of 1967 was more nearly the final than the first step of a change long in the making. The successor regime rejected strict regulation of the states. That had not been the style of the Vocational Rehabilitation Administration or of the Children's Bureau, which had far smaller and less controversial programs than public assistance and which also had closed appropriations. Still less was it the style of the Office of Economic Opportunity, from which Jule Sugarman had just come. All three were different administrative worlds from the old BPA, with its unending stream of state letters and its soberly borne responsibility for millions and then billions of public dollars. Nor was strict regulation the personal style of Mary Switzer, whose well-known contempt for red tape was hailed by a former HEW secretary on the occasion of her appointment to head SRS. She kept in her office a sign bearing Shakespeare's bloody stricture in *Henry VI*: "The first thing we do, let's kill all the lawyers."

As the new regime brought a changed stance toward the states, it brought a parallel change in internal procedure. Decisions once taken in the most elaborate, painstaking way were made more casually. In the BPA/FS even the smallest questions of federal-state relations and the federal sharing of state costs came up for decision to the commissioner—of Social Security between 1935 and 1962, when the BPA was part of the Social Security Administration, and of the Welfare Administration between 1962 and 1967, after the bureau had been separated from the Social Security Administration but before it disappeared into SRS. The office posing an issue or originating a proposal prepared a formal submission that was "practically a legal brief," one veteran of this system recalled. When the commissioner acted, he had this submission before him, along with a covering sheet describing the action recommended and listing the clearances obtained, the information copies distributed, the objections stated by other offices, the reasons for the recommendation, and citations of precedents. Proposed guidance to the states might be circulated to them for comment. Such guidance often went through a dozen or more drafts. The services directives of 1962, an extreme case, were revised thirty-seven times. The commissioner met to consider submissions at regular, stated times. Interested program officials were present, along with representatives of the general counsel's office. The commissioner heard discussion and then announced a decision, which was recorded in formal "action minutes" and circulated. The system exasperated everyone who had to work with it—and ultimately earned their respect, for it fixed responsibility, yielded clear decisions, and compelled as thorough an assessment of the consequences of action as the staff was capable of.

In the new regime, meetings to consider regulations were called on the spur of the moment. Interested persons might or might not be able to come. Discussion proceeded and agreement was apparently reached—but then there would be no record of what had been decided. Whether this less systematic approach affected the content of regulations in 1969 is hard to say. At least the product was published in the *Federal Register* and was plainly enough understood to be policy.[10] The consequences of the disintegration of system would become more apparent a bit later on.

In 1962, when the services legislation was proposed, it had seemed that public assistance might displace vocational rehabilitation. In the end it was more nearly the other way around: vocational rehabilitation took over public assistance and thoroughly changed the administration of services funds.

Not all of the changes in policy in 1969 are attributable to the changed character of administration. The regulations were approved on January 18 by an outgoing Democratic administration, two days before the inauguration of a Republican president. Lame-duck administrations often leave such legacies—important measures designed to advance their own preferences—for their successors to cope with. New regulations at this point no doubt would have followed the course of expansion even had the SRS never been created. For example, the regulations incorporated a broad definition of potential recipients, thus enlarging the population eligible for services.* This was the kind of evolutionary expansion, consistent with BFS principles, that could have been expected to occur even if the old regime had survived. The most important changes in 1969, however, were discontinuous. Departures from precedent, they would not have occurred had not the controlling influence of the BFS been destroyed by reorganization.

Reorganization, it should immediately be added, was not alone the cause of the bureau's loss of control and the development of a wholly different kind of administration. Generational change had weakened the bureau. The founders, who had entered in the depression, were retired or retiring, and those whom this first generation had recruited and indoctrinated in the forties and fifties were nearing retirement. The amendments of 1962 were the last major legislation for which they had much responsibility; by 1967 Wilbur Cohen as under secretary could strike his bargains on the Hill quite free from bureaucratic restraint. Furthermore, the bureau's whole mode of conduct was under strain as welfare case loads grew uncontrollably. Costs soared, and political conflict intensified. Fresh claimants demanded the right to share in

---

* The regulations covering service programs for families and children defined potential recipients as those families and children who:

(i) Are eligible for medical assistance, as medically needy persons, under the State [Medicaid] plan.

(ii) Would be eligible for financial assistance if the earnings exemption granted to recipients applied to them.

(iii) Are likely, within 5 years, to become recipients of financial assistance.

(iv) Are at or near dependency level, including those in low-income neighborhoods and among other groups that might otherwise include more AFDC cases, where services are provided on a group basis.

(*Federal Register*, vol. 34 [January 28, 1969], p. 1360.)

making welfare policy—not just recipient groups and radical activists, who were newly mobilized in the 1960s, but politicians, starting with the President of the United States, who had traditionally ignored public assistance and now found that they could ignore it no longer. Professional, bureaucratic dominance was bound to give way under these pressures.

It is arguable that, as the stakes of the program rose, careful administrative controls were more necessary than ever, but they were also more difficult to achieve, and the bureau's efforts to achieve them now appeared futile or worse to the program's growing number of critics. The regulatory mode had produced an enormous amount of red tape. Paperwork was the curse of the caseworker, the curse of the whole program. Yet strict control had not stopped the mounting tide of cases. Superficially, public assistance certainly did not seem to be well controlled. And even if none of these external pressures had been at work on the bureau, it would have been in trouble specifically over services, an activity inherently hard to define and therefore not amenable to the bureau's customary regulation.

It was not just the habit of careful staff work that had caused the bureau to go through thirty-seven drafts of services regulations in 1961–62. It was the extreme difficulty of instructing the states on so problematic a subject, whose concrete meaning depended on the individual worker's exercise of discretion. In the eyes of its critics, what the bureau resorted to—case load and visiting standards—epitomized the arbitrariness of administration by narrowly specialized professionals. Rational men who were not graduates of a school of social work found it hard to see what was sacred about one worker for every sixty cases or one home visit every three months, or whatever. It did not help that the profession, social work, could make no persuasive claim to possessing an esoteric skill or body of knowledge. Nor did it help that services, as the bureau had conceived of them, had not gotten people off welfare. The promises of 1962 in that respect had turned out to be false.[11] In short, the bureau was in trouble in the 1960s, the social work profession was under attack, and the reorganization was in some measure a response.

CHAPTER FOUR

Political Demand
and Governmental Decentralization

To UNDERSTAND why services spending got so completely out of control, it is necessary to look beyond the law and its administration to the state of the country and of the government generally. Two conditions are particularly pertinent. One was a high level of political demand for government benefits. As Daniel P. Moynihan has put it, "The idea of limits was not much in fashion."[1] The other was governmental decentralization. The idea that the federal government should closely control state and local governments was not in fashion either.

Like the 1930s, the 1960s were years in which the domestic activity of the federal government took a large leap. So, it may be supposed, did the expectations of those who had come to depend on federal benefits. Increasingly, the country was tutored to turn to Washington.

Grants-in-aid to the states are nearly as old as our federal form of government, but only recently have they come to figure importantly in the conduct of state and local governments. As the volume of grants grew in the 1960s, state and local chief executives learned that the federal government defined their range of initiative. If they wanted to do something new, they would need Washington's sponsorship or help. If they needed new revenue, again they learned to look to Washington —by no means exclusively, for they continued to develop tax sources in their own jurisdictions, but federal help was now an option to be automatically considered. To secure more federal funds, the biggest state and city governments set up Washington offices, and all learned to use such organizations as the Council of State Governments or the Conference of Mayors, whose staffs in the capital grew. Back home, state and local chief executives learned the value of—and competed for—administrators who could win their share and more of Washington's funds. If federal law created an opportunity, as in the services case, by the late 1960s at least some state governments had acquired the capacity for detecting it.

As traditional claimants were acquiring new perceptions and skills, new groups of claimants were appearing. Federal action fostered a number of organizations in the 1960s that were established more or less for the purpose of making claims on the federal government—typically, on behalf of disadvantaged constituencies. Model cities agencies, inspired by the Demonstration Cities and Metropolitan Development Act of 1966, were for this purpose precisely; they were supposed to attract more funds to the poverty-stricken areas of central cities. Similarly, the Appalachian Regional Commission (ARC) had been created in 1965 to serve as an official advocate in Washington on behalf of a poor region. Such organizations were dedicated to detecting opportunities of the kind that federal law presented in the case of services grants. The ARC started a child development program in 1969 partly to encourage the thirteen Appalachian states to make use of services funds.

Not all grantsmen were governmental. A private consulting industry had developed to market the knowledge and skills with which to secure federal grants. Individual entrepreneurs rather than the big consulting firms detected the possibilities in services grants. The first of these to become active, William Copeland, noticed the potential of services funding while working on comprehensive health planning in Pennsylvania in 1967–68. Copeland's intellectual interests were eclectic (biostatistics, theology, clinical psychology, and intellectual history, studied at the universities of Chicago, Pittsburgh, and Minnesota), and so was his career. He had been a staff member or consultant with various public or quasi-public organizations, including the American Public Welfare Association, the American Rehabilitation Association, the Public Health Service, and other elements of the Department of Health, Education, and Welfare (HEW). Though he had no advanced degree, Copeland had an intellectual bent; he tended to think abstractly. He liked to conceive of intergovernmental relations as a mathematical model constructed to yield the maximum return in federal funds to a given state. He put his hypothesis this way: "Question: If every state commissioner went to his federal counterpart and got all he could, would the state have maximized federal funding? Answer: No. There has to be interagency funding." He was also didactic. Addressing state officials, he wrote: "The first important thing to understand is the Theory of Matching Ratios. While the mathematical properties of ratios and proportions may be confusing or boring, depending upon the mathematical ability of the reader, the fact remains that knowing how they work is worth millions of dollars to the people of a State. The writer has seen small States losing ten to twenty millions of dollars per year because they did not understand the subject." By the end of 1968 Copeland was prepared to explain his ideas about services funding to state or local governments that engaged his services. HEW aided him in this. His paper, "Financing Rehabilitation Services," which explained in considerable detail how the states might maximize services grants, was published in 1969 and sold by the Government Printing Office for 25 cents. Copeland's activity retained a quasi-public character.[2]

Taking office in 1969, the Nixon administration meant to deflate expectations and discourage demand. While it did not immediately eliminate any of the large legacy of fresh Democratic programs such as model cities, it did begin to make cuts. As one source of funds would dry up, recipients and associated grantsmen would cast about for another. Casting about, they could find services grants, "the one well that still ran," as one close observer put it. This juxtaposition of high demand and decreasing supply from other sources made the potential of services grants all the more important and attractive.

The proliferation of categorical grants in the 1960s produced another reaction, too, in the form of governmental measures that loosened federal restrictions on the states. Like heightened demand for federal benefits, this move toward decentralization was an important element of the context in which services spending grew.

By the close of the decade it was the conventional wisdom in Washington that categorical grant programs had become too complicated in the course of their recent haphazard growth. There were too many categories of aid, and many of the categories were thought to incorporate excessive controls. Reformers of federal administration set out to rationalize grants by eliminating controls, consolidating categories, and in general moving toward the provision of money on more permissive terms. Beginning as management doctrine under the Democrats, this approach proved thoroughly congenial after 1969 to the newly arrived Republicans, who were ideologically more disposed toward decentralization than the Democrats. The Nixon proposals for revenue sharing carried decentralization further than the Johnson administration had proposed to take it.

The Intergovernmental Cooperation Act of 1968 was an early product of the attempt to rationalize and decentralize grant-in-aid programs, and one of its provisions proved to be important in the making of the loophole for services spending. Section 204 of that act authorized federal department heads to waive the statutory requirement that "a single state agency" be in charge of administering the federal grant. The single-state-agency requirement had been dogma for the Bureau of Family Services (BFS), and was the bureau's main technique for securing accountability for the expenditure of federal funds. Reform from outside the administering agency now weakened that traditional instrument of central control. Here again, as in the reorganization that had created the Social and Rehabilitation Service, one object of reform was to increase the power of generalist officials in relation to specialists. The proponents of the Intergovernmental Cooperation Act were management officials in the Bureau of the Budget, in combination with the Government Operations committees in Congress and the Advisory Commission on Intergovernmental Relations; together they operated on the theory that professional specialists had grown too powerful through the medium of narrowly specialized grant programs, which the specialists dominated from top to bottom of the federal system.[3] The reformers sought to assert the primacy of generalist staffs at all levels of government in the federal system and at all levels of the hierarchy in the federal government's administrative structure. To this school of thought, single-state-agency requirements unduly restricted the governor's freedom to organize his own administration.

Probably more important than any concrete measure of decentralization, however, was the creation of a climate in which some HEW officials could rationalize the unsupervised flow of services funds to the states. Having made several proposals to grant the states funds on highly permissive terms, President Nixon had lent legitimacy to the practice within his administration.

CHAPTER FIVE

Leading Case Number One: California

A LOOSE LAW, the changed character of administration, the rising demand for federal benefits, the development of a reform doctrine of greater federal responsiveness to the states—all these were conditions antecedent to the explosion of services spending, conditions that made the explosion highly probable but still do not fully explain it. For the outburst actually to occur, the state governments had to take certain specific steps. They had to make their claims and have them approved by federal administrators. The first and for several years the only state to do this in a big way was California.

From 1967 through 1971, as the following breakdown shows, California received 25 to 36 percent of the federal grants for social services and training:[1]

Fiscal year	Total grants (thousands of dollars)	Grants to California (thousands of dollars)	Percent of total grants to California
1967	241,567	59,907	25
1968	295,094	86,367	30
1969	396,691	143,229	36
1970	689,062	205,068	30
1971	776,221	216,633	28

It began drawing heavily on services funds even before the 1967 amendments, and when the subsequent change in federal policy occurred California detected it promptly. "There was something from California all the time," a retired official of the Bureau of Family Services (BFS) recalled. "They were clever. It got so you had to look at everything with a jaundiced eye. You never knew where anything was going to lead you with California."

California relied on no single technique for exploiting services grants. It culled the rules and designed responses to fit. When the BFS instructed state agencies to help remove inmates from mental institutions, California transferred several hundred workers from the Department of Mental Hygiene to the Department of Social Welfare, qualifying the state to receive 75 percent federal matching for their salaries. This was in 1966. Three years after the 1962 amendments authorized purchase, California enacted a preschool compensatory education program based on that technique, and when federal administrators began promoting purchase after 1967, California's Department of Social Welfare immediately instructed county welfare departments to purchase everything they could.

Activities that were already being performed—such as attendant care for infirm persons or day care for children receiving benefits under Aid to Families with Dependent Children (AFDC)—were now provided in such a way as to maximize federal money. Not only were attendants paid with 75 percent matching funds, but welfare recipients were designated as attendants so that the federal share of their support could be increased from the usual 50 percent. For example, if an elderly couple were both on welfare and one needed attendant care, the spouse could be designated the attendant—the service-provider—and the state-local share of income support could be reduced accordingly. State laws were drafted to facilitate the receipt of federal matching funds. The Unruh Preschool Act of 1965, in establishing the preschool compensatory education program, defined it as a social service for children receiving AFDC and subject to the 75 percent rate of federal financial participation authorized by Title IV of the Social Security Act; the legislature appropriated funds to the Department of Social Welfare specifically to cover the nonfederal share of this service. That was typical. With regard to attendant care, an amendment in 1968 expressed the legislature's intention that welfare recipients receive priority in employment as attendants.[2]

How much of the federal money went for new services and how much replaced state-local effort would be hard to establish, even program by program. Consider the case of California's children's centers, day-care facilities set up during World War II for children of working

mothers. Started with federal help, these centers had been continued
even though federal funds ended with the war. Since 1947 the state had
been paying two-thirds of the cost and the parents one-third, with individual fees adjusted to parent income through a sliding scale. In 1968
the state legislature authorized county welfare departments to pay the
children's centers for day care of current, former, and potential welfare
recipients under the services matching provisions of the Social Security
Act at a rate that would secure the maximum return in federal funds.
As a state legislative report explained, the intent of the law "was to
substitute as much federal money as possible for state and local financing of Children's Center care, and to make the state General Fund
savings available to the State Department of Social Welfare for financing additional day care . . . total Children's Center funding would be
unaffected, but some federal funds would be substituted for state funds,
and these state funds would be used to earn additional federal funds for
day-care expansion."[3] In fact, state, local, and private funding of the
children's centers remained fairly stable between fiscal years 1968 and
1971, while federal participation rose from zero to $12.7 million, as
shown below (in millions of dollars):[4]

	1968	1969	1970	1971
Federal	. . .	2,351,249	10,932,365	12,734,882
State, local, other	18,127,833	20,948,352	16,789,646	19,751,210

The number of children served rose from 15,477 to 20,700. Whether
federal aid substituted for state effort or enlarged services is problematic.
It appears to have done some of both in this particular program; the
indirect effects on other programs are not traceable.[5]

California officials had a sophisticated grasp of the implications of
the open end in social services and of the ways in which private as well
as state and local public funds could be used to tap it. A legislative staff
report early in 1969 recommended that the state Department of Rehabilitation be redesignated the Department of Social and Rehabilitation Services and given responsibility for all social service functions, an
arrangement that would facilitate the fullest use of services grants. The
report is worth quoting at length on this point, to show how fully
and forthrightly California had elaborated the strategy:

There are three major financing mechanisms for social and rehabilitation services which should be fully utilized before additional state funds are appropriated. They are: 1) Section 2 of Public Law 565 (the basic federal rehabilitation law), 2) the 1962 Social Service Amendments to the Social Security Act, and 3) welfare aid presently being paid recipients. We propose to deploy these existing expenditures in a way which will produce an optimum return of federal dollars for a minimum amount of state and local dollars. The Department of Rehabilitation would reevaluate each program it now administers with the goal of seeking alternative methods of financing those programs.

Presently, nearly all of the rehabilitation programs are being financed under Section 2 (the basic rehabilitation finance section) of PL 83-565 at a federal-state ratio of 75%–25%. Unlike the Social Service Amendments to the Social Security Act, this provision has a federal dollar ceiling which automatically limits the amount of state or local funds that can be matched by the federal government. The Social Service Amendments, however, have no federal ceiling.

The first task would be to shift existing rehabilitation services that would qualify under the Service Amendments, such as counseling and guidance testing, from rehabilitation funding to the Social Service Amendments, thus freeing federal rehabilitation dollars. This could be facilitated by combining the State Department of Vocational Rehabilitation Services and the service functions of the Department of Social Welfare.

The new combined department would be known as the Department of Social and Rehabilitation Services and would facilitate maximum use of limited rehabilitation dollars. All functions now performed by the State Department of Vocational Rehabilitation which could be considered public social services would be matched by unlimited federal social service funds. The proposed State Department of Social and Rehabilitation Services would claim matching money from limited federal Vocational Rehabilitation funds only for specialized rehabilitation functions which would not be eligible for federal social services reimbursement. In other words, Vocational Rehabilitation specialists would not use up limited federal matching dollars to provide services which could receive matching funds from the unlimited pool. In this way, federal rehabilitation funds could be reserved for persons who may be ineligible for public social services because they lack a connection with a federally aided assistance program.[6]

The same report also recommended creating an intergovernmental and interdepartmental services fund, again for the purpose of managing funds to maximize federal matching. The report explained that private agencies would also be able to participate to their advantage, in a passage notable for its explication of the fiscal strategy:

By investing their funds in the Intergovernmental and Interdepartmental

Service Fund the voluntary agencies would obtain federal matching funds, too.

Recent federal legislation offers the potential for improving the planning and funding of private social services. The 1967 Amendments to the Social Security Act permit public welfare agencies, for the first time, to contract directly with non-public agencies for social services. This makes it possible for the public agencies not only to utilize a larger supply of services but also to expand the funding base of these services. The latter can be accomplished by having the private non-profit agencies agree to allocate their funds as the non-federal share of costs of services which they will provide under contract.

Such private agency investments would have to fit into the overall service plan for the public system. However, there are many reasons, ranging from interest in the poor to the desire to present coordinated private services, which indicate that it would be advantageous to the voluntary agencies to enter into such arrangements. The most obvious attraction of the plan, of course, is the increased funding which federal matching formulas would provide.

Once the voluntary agency has invested its funds in the central account, the Department of Social and Rehabilitation Services would then contract with that agency to provide its specialized service. For example, a private agency earmarking from its budget the funds that will support one worker if only private funds are available, can augment that amount with 75% federal matching funds, or enough money to employ a total of four workers —provided, of course, that services are directed to persons who qualify for matching funds. This expansion of available service funds would be accomplished at no additional cost to the state or county.[7]

To maximize federal grants, California took fairly obvious steps— steps that a close reading of the federal rules would have suggested to men who read them with that purpose in view. California is remarkable more for the way in which the state government proceeded than in what it did. The degree of legislative initiative is striking.

By and large grantsmen have operated from offices in the executive branch or private consulting firms under contract to executive agencies. California was different in that initiatives came from legislative staffs that had been built up in the 1960s under the leadership of a powerful and ambitious speaker of the Assembly, Jesse Unruh. One staff member in particular was responsible for the state's enterprise in regard to service grants. He was Thomas C. W. Joe, who came to the legislature in 1961 as a graduate student in political theory at Berkeley, on a Ford Foundation internship that gave students practical experience. Joe quit graduate study and stayed through 1968 as a staff specialist on welfare.

To an exceptional degree he had the grantsman's gifts of detecting possibilities in the rules and daring to propose their exploitation. (His mastery of the rules was the more remarkable in that he was blind.) A Democrat and a liberal, fully committed to enlarging public aid for the poor, he prepared the preschool program for Speaker Unruh and worked successfully in tandem for several years with John G. Veneman, a liberal Republican from a Democratic district who at that time was a member of the Assembly Committee on Social Welfare and chairman of the Joint Committee on Medi-Cal (Medicaid) Administration. With the legislature more than supporting them, indeed showing the way, administrators in the California Department of Social Welfare had a license to organize and enlarge their activities so as to capture services grants.

Federal regional officials were fully informed of California's actions. They met regularly with executives of the state welfare department who were in charge of social services. They cleared the state's proposals with Washington headquarters, and headquarters imposed no restraints. Ordinarily, state officials had a clearer perception than did federal regional officials of what the Social and Rehabilitation Service (SRS) headquarters would approve. "We had a better pipeline than they did," a California official recalled. "It became a joke." Federal regional officials would seek policy interpretation from state officials instead of the other way around. Initiative lay with the state. "It would have been difficult to have a regional staff that could stand up to them," according to a veteran member of the central staff. Certainly no regional staff could stand up to California without backing from headquarters, and such backing, which was not always firm even before the reorganization, crumbled altogether when the SRS was created.

With California drawing so heavily on services funds, it was only a matter of time before other states would learn from the example. Conceivably, however, a conservative administration after 1969 might have forestalled state action by reversing the expansionist course of federal policy. When it did not, the way was open for massive state claims.

CHAPTER SIX

The Change of Administrations

THE CHANGE in party control of the executive branch brought no change in executive attitudes toward social services within the Department of Health, Education, and Welfare (HEW). If anything, the changes in leadership and organization that occurred in 1969–70 encouraged expansion.

As the Nixon administration began, California came to Washington. Lieutenant Governor Robert H. Finch was named secretary of HEW. More to the point of this story, John Veneman came with him as under secretary, and both under Finch and Elliot Richardson, who succeeded Finch in the summer of 1970, Veneman oversaw policy planning and the administration of services and other welfare programs. More to the point still, Veneman brought with him as special assistant Tom Joe, who took a keen interest in the evolution of services spending. In 1968 Joe had written "Finding Welfare Dollars," a paper for the American Public Welfare Association, which financed his work with a grant from the Office of Economic Opportunity. Traveling outside California, he had met a number of state and local officials and William Copeland, who became a friend and later, after Joe had left HEW, a business partner. Arriving in Washington in 1969 as an expert in securing grants for the states, Joe did not change roles as much as might have been expected. On the phone or with state and local officials who stopped to see him at the department, he continued to give advice on how to use services grants. He did so with Veneman's approval or, on occasion, with his active participation. In "Finding Welfare Dollars," Joe declared that the public welfare system is the major source of financing programs for the poor. "The aim," he wrote, "is to maximize the total resources available to the poorest segment of our society . . . in each state, the potential ability to fill the gaps in human services for the poor . . . *depends heavily on how a variety of state and local dollar investments are articulated with the resources of the existing public welfare programs.*"[1]

Mary Switzer remained administrator of the Social and Rehabilitation Service (SRS) until March 1970, when she was succeeded by John D. Twiname, who had been her deputy for a year. A Nixon appointee with a degree from the Harvard Business School and experience in private management, Twiname did not fit what was to become the stereotype of the Nixon administration's managerial man. He was not tough. Subordinates found him charming, amiable, and thoroughly well-intentioned. In regard to policy, his instincts were liberal. Appeals to the well-being of the poor always moved him. Distinctly a business-man with a social conscience, he listed the following activities in his official biographical sketch:

Founding member and president of the Board of Chicago Business-Industrial Project, one of the first "industrial missions" in the United States. Project was organized to bring together leaders of business, labor, the black community, plus university and Government people, to focus on social problems; board member, Wilmette Human Relations Committee; cochairman, fund raising task force for ghetto self-help project "Toward Responsible Freedom" (project of community renewal society); Chicago Executives Club; Economic Club of Chicago.[2]

Under Twiname, as under Switzer, the SRS continued to push the expansion of social services, while organizationally the effort to develop the administrator's staff and to assert generalist control over the professional specialists in subunits of the SRS continued, sustained by advice from a management consulting firm. If there was any perceptible change with the arrival of a Republican appointee, it was in the greater emphasis put on "management," but critics of Twiname's administration of the SRS thought that there was more rhetoric than reality in this. One such critic came away from the SRS remembering a particularly meaningless phrase from a manpower utilization report: "The common theme [in the SRS] is the pursuit of an elusive synergism." It stuck in his mind, epitomizing SRS leadership in the first years of this Republican managerial era. To this observer, the top of the SRS seemed all caught up with "fluff stuff," such as management by objectives and cross-bureau planning, and not given to asking the hard, straightforward questions, such as how much money are we spending, what is it going for, is that what we intend it should go for, and if not, should we revise our policies? Asked of services spending, such questions would not have yielded satisfying answers.

In the fall of 1969 one organizational change occurred that might have improved administrative supervision of services grants. The Community Services Administration (CSA), a new subunit of the SRS, was created with an appointive head "to provide a focal point for development of improved methods of social service delivery, improve management of social service programs, and provide for better communitywide planning and coordination of these services."[3] Coming late to the scene, the CSA had a hard time getting under way. Its staff was small—85 or 90 in the central office, including clerical positions—and "twice culled," as one observer put it. In the 1967 reorganization, services personnel of the Bureau of Family Services had been scattered to the various program units of the SRS. Now they were brought together again—what was left of them from the continuing exodus of experienced personnel. Parts of the Children's Bureau were also included in the CSA, while the rest constituted the core of a new Office of Child Development (OCD), which was located in the Office of the Secretary and given responsibility for administering Head Start and research and program development. Observers within the department thought that the OCD got more than its share of the Children's Bureau's best qualified specialists in family and children's services. As an attempt by the SRS to consolidate responsibility for services, the CSA was only a partial success. Because CSA began as the compromise product of a conflict between SRS executives and Jule Sugarman over where services functions should be located and in a setting of persistent organizational turmoil and uncertainty for career personnel, it was demoralized from the start. Or so it seemed to one career official who subsequently remarked sardonically that he was a member of the CSA's PODO club—he had been "present on day one."

If the CSA as a whole was little able to supervise spending, it was not much encouraged to do so from the top. The first administrator was a Democratic holdover and professional social worker, Stephen P. Simonds, who had formerly headed the Assistance Payments Administration. Liked by his subordinates in the CSA as a man of decency and integrity, he was nonetheless not regarded as a good administrator. He was "not the best organized guy in the world," as one said, nor was he inclined to master provisions of policy or methods of supervision. The general attitude at the top of the CSA, then and for several years afterward, was that since services spending benefited the poor it should be encouraged to develop in anticipation of the day when someone managed to limit it. The attitude of the CSA leadership was essentially promotional, which was perhaps inevitable in a new organization created for the purpose of overseeing a services program and blessed with the opportunity embodied in the open end.

The one major attempt at revising services policies in 1969–70 developed outside the SRS in the offices of the HEW secretary, more or less incident to the planning of the Family Assistance Plan (FAP), the Nixon administration's income maintenance proposal. The FAP was submitted to Congress in the fall of 1969, and the closing paragraph of Secretary Finch's long explanatory statement promised that HEW would follow with a legislative proposal in regard to services. Nine months later, the proposal was submitted to Congress as part of a revised version of the FAP.[4]

The administration's services proposal resembled various Nixon special revenue-sharing plans in that it was designed to merge federal categories of aid. It would have given governors and mayors powers to transfer up to 20 percent of federal funds between any HEW-funded service programs that they included in a consolidated plan—a "kind of revenue sharing," Secretary Finch said, which "would give State and local governments the flexibility to tailor Federal dollars to their own priorities."[5] The proposal would also have closed the open end by authorizing a specific level of annual appropriations, and it would have allocated funds among the states by a statutory formula.

The preparation of this proposal was one more sign of the decline of specialist control over services. Legislative planning in 1962, when services provisions of the Social Security Act were introduced, had conformed to a pattern developed over the decades since the New Deal. The bureau that was to administer the legislation did the planning for it and stamped the law with the conceptual preferences of the particular profession that staffed that bureau. Subsequently, reorganization within HEW dispersed administrative responsibility for services among several units of the SRS. There was no bureau in charge of services until the CSA was created in the fall of 1969; weakest of the SRS subunits, the CSA did not fill the vacuum. Meanwhile, responsibility for legislative planning for domestic programs was being transferred from operating bureaus to secretarial staffs in the departments and to the Executive Office of the President. The Nixon administration made a particular effort to centralize program planning in HEW at the departmental level.[6] The Office of the Assistant Secretary for Planning and Evaluation oversaw preparation of the services proposal of 1970. Thereafter the proposal was reviewed by a task force consisting of a White House staff member, an assistant director of the Office of Management and Budget, and a representative of the Department of Labor as well as HEW's deputy under secretary for policy.[7] One of John Twiname's first acts as administrator of the SRS was to protest the exclusion of his organization from services planning. "Thank you for hearing me out on Thursday," he wrote to HEW's deputy under secretary for management and the assistant secretary for planning and evaluation. "I hope I didn't overstate the case for participation . . . by the operating heads. It is a little more trouble in the beginning but saves a lot of alienation down the line later on."[8] In the end the administration's proposal was distinctly that of central planners, characteristically seeking to rationalize a multitude of overlapping programs and methods of fund distribution.

Nothing came of the proposal. The House Ways and Means Committee incorporated very little of it in the committee version of the Family Assistance Plan, and that little—which would have closed the open end at $800 million for fiscal year 1973—went down with the parent bill, which passed the House in 1971 but had no chance in the Senate. The department's great preoccupation with achieving the FAP, then, did not foster services legislation as a by-product, and it may well have encouraged the SRS to pursue an expansionist course in regard to services if only to protect its own future. The SRS would not have administered the Family Assistance Plan, nor did administration planning call for it to administer the Family Health Insurance Plan, which would have replaced Medicaid. If SRS lost these programs, services would be the only thing left, and in 1970 they were a very small fraction of its $9.5 billion budget.[9]

Quite apart from a willingness to support services spending for its own sake, the new Republican administration of HEW brought to the department a strong interest in directing federal aid away from functional specialists toward general purpose elements of state and local governments, and services grants were attractive as a way to do this, since— through the vagueness of statutory language and the vicissitudes of

HEW's internal reorganizations—they had been cut loose from specialist control. HEW's Center for Community Planning, a small unit in the Office of the Assistant Secretary for Community and Field Services, was particularly concerned after 1969 with diverting the department's funds out of specialized channels; as a concrete instance, it was charged with finding HEW funds for model cities programs. One member of this office, Rocco D'Amico, who had formerly worked with William Copeland in the American Rehabilitation Foundation, spent much of his time between late 1969 and the summer of 1971 encouraging model cities agencies to make use of social services grants. Later, after Richardson had taken over as secretary, this office worked on a piece of proposed legislation, the Allied Services Act of 1972, which would have encouraged state and local governments to consolidate the planning and implementation of social service programs. Coming to the department in mid-1970 with long experience of its programs, Richardson attached the highest importance to combating the parochialism of the professional specialists; in his view, what services programs needed above all was better coordination among the providers of service.[10]

With no change in federal policy, services spending doubled in the first two years of the Nixon administration, rising from $396.6 million in fiscal year 1969 to $776.2 million in 1971. In the states, growth was uneven. California continued to get a disproportionate share. In Oregon, Washington, and Pennsylvania, services spending grew at several times the national rate. (In Oregon, an extreme case, the jump was from $2.4 million to $24.6 million.) How much a state benefited could depend not only on its enterprise but also on its fortune in making connections with consultants or on the advice it got from regional officials. Copeland was very active in Hennepin County, Minnesota, which helps to account for the tripling of grants to that state. Copeland, some of his associates in the American Rehabilitation Foundation, and Tom Joe, before Joe went to HEW, had been active in Pennsylvania.[11] Some regional officials —especially in Region IV (Atlanta)—encouraged the states to act, whereas others were passive.

In regard to services spending, decentralization within the federal administration was real; regional officials could exercise discretion. Departmental reform in the late 1960s had this as an objective, and the Nixon administration was trying hard to decentralize administration in all of the domestic departments. Yet the decentralization in administration of services grants was more the result of disintegration in SRS head-quarters than of successfully planned change. Decentralization occurred by default. There was no centralization, which is to say no organization in Washington capable of giving clear, sustained, and consistent administrative instructions. This put a considerable burden of decision on the ten regional units, which might solicit guidance from headquarters, but, if they did, were likely to get ad hoc replies only. The lack of a policy-making capacity and a systematic procedure in the CSA also meant that headquarters was open to manipulation by regional officials, who could seek the advice they wanted to hear. Region IV, which was strongly encouraging the states to make use of services grants, would get advice by phone directly from the commissioner's office, which was likely to give casual, affirmative responses. Other regions, more concerned to stay within bounds, would solicit written responses from the technical staff. Regional offices might or might not obtain cost estimates along with the states' proposals of a social services plan. Headquarters did not require such estimates. Not until state plans were approved and state claims for matching funds actually began to be made did the SRS discover what fiscal commitments its regional offices collectively had made.

Regional offices reflected the parent organization in that their staffs were small (35 staff members nationwide, an average of 3.5 per region), newly assembled, and short on experience in administering the federal public assistance program. A nationwide reorganization of federal regional offices, the result of the Nixon administration's decision to create ten standard administrative regions for the major domestic agencies, in some places contributed an additional element of instability. The following recollection of a federal official in Philadelphia, associate regional commissioner for community services from 1970 to 1972, is indicative:

I came to work for the Department in September of 1970, and I was brand new to Federal Service. I had never worked in the Federal Agency, or for that matter in any State Welfare Agency, and, of course—well, the position I came to, the Regional Office had moved from Charlottesville, Virginia. There were several people who didn't come up with it. There were vacancies. I came to work for the Department. Of course, there was a tremendous amount to be learned—you know, the whole world of Federal Regulations and State relationships was just an enormous thing to take on, and I did, to the best of my ability. We had a very meager staff in the Regional Office. There were, I think, two of us, or maybe three of us in the Community Services Unit. As the Chief of Community Services, I was responsible for the Federal role in the development of Social Services for the children's and adults' categories of the Social Security Act.

Now, in addition to all that I had to learn, I nonetheless felt that there were certain practices and procedures that I just couldn't understand, no matter how much I dug in. I had been a social worker in a variety of very responsible social work positions, some of which have been of an administrative nature, and I had major questions about the whole money business, huge agreements, purchasing services between the State Agency, and a private procedure, which no one in our office would know anything about. The monies for these social services just went through a regular grant award agreement. Nobody ever took a look, it seemed to me, to see what was happening, or whether or not the money was really being spent. . . .[12]

CHAPTER SEVEN

Leading Case Number Two:
Illinois

THE STATE that touched off the spending explosion of 1972 was Illinois, which advanced a bold interpretation of federal regulations on the purchase of services and precipitated a fresh and permissive statement of federal policy. With the actions of Illinois, social services spending emerged as an issue of high politics. The Illinois demands engaged the personal attention of the President, involved the governor's office in a confrontation with the Office of Management and Budget, and culminated in a victory for the state on the floor of the Senate.

Illinois was one of many states in which budgets were badly strained by rising welfare costs. In a typical report, one news magazine declared early in 1971 that welfare spending was threatening to bankrupt the states and cities. "Many Governors and mayors," according to *U.S. News and World Report*, "regard the soaring costs of the public-assistance and medical programs as the most crucial domestic problem in the nation today."[1] Governors cracked down at home and called on Washington to help.

In Illinois, coping with the welfare and fiscal crisis was up to a progressive Republican governor, Richard B. Ogilvie, who had been elected simultaneously with President Nixon in 1968, and to the very able, well-educated young men whom he had attracted to his staff. Most of this staff was located in the newly formed, eighty-man Bureau of the Budget, patterned after the federal one and, like it, designed to assist the chief executive with program and fiscal planning. The director of the Illinois bureau was John W. McCarter, Jr., a graduate of the Harvard Business School who had been with the management consulting firm of Booz, Allen and Hamilton before being named a White House

43

fellow in 1966–67. As a White House fellow, he was assigned to assist Budget Director Charles L. Schultze. He occupied the connecting office between Schultze and Deputy Director Phillip S. Hughes—not a bad vantage point from which to learn the workings of the federal executive branch. McCarter's deputy, John F. Cotton, likewise had Washington experience. A physicist turned systems analyst, he had worked in the Office of the Secretary of Defense, collaborated with the economist Selma Mushkin on introducing planning, programming, and budgeting systems into state governments, and had briefly been in Vermont in the Democratic administration of Governor Philip Hoff. The budget staff specialist on public assistance, Ogilvie's principal adviser on the subject, was George A. Ranney, Jr., member of a wealthy and public-spirited Chicago family who had worked in a legal services agency as well as a private law firm after getting his bachelor's degree from Harvard and a law degree from the University of Chicago. (After his service to Ogilvie was over, Ranney became general counsel of the family firm, Inland Steel.)

In the fall of 1970, as McCarter, Cotton, and their staff prepared the budget for fiscal year 1972, they foresaw a sizable deficit, on the order of $140 million, as the result mainly of rising welfare costs. The governor and his staff were determined not to make up this deficit at the expense of the poor by cutting welfare grants. They decided not to let such grants fall below the state-defined standard of need and not to cancel automatic adjustments for the rise in the cost of living. (If state employees got such increases, the Ogilvie administration reasoned, so should welfare recipients.) There was "a terrific commitment" not to cut grants, one staff member recalled; this became the touchstone of the Ogilvie administration's liberalism. For Ranney in particular, it was virtually a condition for his remaining on the staff. And, unwilling to cut welfare grants, Ogilvie and his staff were downright unable, so they believed, to raise taxes. Ogilvie had begun his term that way, by securing the first income tax in Illinois, and it had cost him heavily. Down in the polls, in danger of losing the 1972 election or even of being dumped by the Republican party, he was in no position to go to the legislature or the public again. He and his staff concluded that they must make up their deficit with federal funds.[2] If this caused problems for the Nixon administration, it was too bad. Ogilvie's staff thought of themselves as "Ogilvie Republicans," which was not quite the same as being

Republicans. Ogilvie himself had some sense that the President was very much in his debt. He had supported Nixon at the 1968 Republican convention and believed that otherwise Nixon might not have gotten the nomination. Within Illinois, the Ogilvie administration tried to trade on its party affiliation with the national administration and on the Washington experience of the governor's staff. The Ogilvie administration let it be known that, with their Washington connections, they could be counted on to deliver. If they failed to deliver, they would be badly embarrassed and discredited back home.

At about the time that Illinois budget officials were making their plans for fiscal year 1972—that is, in the fall of 1970—they discovered the possibilities in social services grants, and on December 30, 1970, they submitted several major amendments to the Illinois plan for social services to Donald F. Simpson, the regional commissioner of the Social and Rehabilitation Service (SRS) in Chicago. They then proceeded to base their 1972 budget on the assumption that the Department of Health, Education, and Welfare (HEW) would approve and fund these proposals, yielding the state an additional $75 million in federal aid. Beyond that, they also assumed that $65 million in new federal funds would come from the Family Assistance Plan (FAP) or some other fresh source, presumably revenue sharing, which Governor Ogilvie had actively supported.[3]

Bold as a budgeting tactic, the Illinois social service proposals were bolder still in what they contained. In fully exploiting the loophole that federal laws, rules, and administrative practice had opened, Illinois went well beyond what California or any other state had done.

Illinois proposed that its Department of Public Aid should make substantial purchases of service from other state agencies, including Mental Health and Corrections. These purchases would cover part of the cost of state programs dealing with drug abuse, alcoholism, mental illness, mental retardation, and juvenile and adult corrections. Purchase, of course, was not new, but in the main it was being used for day care, consistent with the federal intent expressed in 1967.[4] Booz, Allen and Hamilton, an SRS consultant, concluded early in 1971 that the great bulk of purchased service was for that purpose—$63.3 million out of $79.9 million in the three states studied (California, Pennsylvania, and Wisconsin, which were the leading practitioners of purchase). Indeed, $48 million of the $63 million was accounted for by three contracts—

two in California, for the preschool compensatory program and for the children's centers, and one in Pennsylvania, for a day-care program for which the state public welfare department had contracted with the Philadelphia schools. The contracts that were not for day care were mostly small (under $100,000), localized, and tailored to the offerings of particular private agencies and the needs of particular recipients. They covered, for example, services for unwed parents, family counseling, foster care and adoptions, emergency shelter and protection, and homemakers—all traditionally provided by private sources.[5] By contrast, Illinois was proposing to purchase from other state agencies, in large amounts, for a number of purposes other than day care, including purposes that were long-established responsibilities of the state governments.

The specter that had troubled veteran public assistance administrators—that the states would exploit the open end for the purpose of fiscal relief, simply to transfer ongoing costs to the federal government—was raised by the Illinois plan. That the proposals were initiated by the Budget Bureau substantiated this interpretation. Technically, the proposals were submitted by the director of the Department of Public Aid, Harold O. Swank, but he was a reluctant collaborator in what he regarded as a dubious venture; Ogilvie would soon seek to replace him.

Some of the language in the Illinois proposals seemed to suggest that state programs would expand with federal services funds. The Ogilvie administration was trying in general to enlarge social programs in what was traditionally a low-spending state. (The very strength of their commitment to reform and their confidence in their own liberalism increased the assurance of Ogilvie's staff that what they were doing in regard to services was right.) But there was no promise in the Illinois submission that state effort would increase, nor was there any reason to make such a promise. Neither federal law nor the 1969 regulations required it. Besides citing the broad language of federal laws and rules in regard to the definition of services, former and potential recipients, and group eligibility, Illinois officials did try to establish a logical connection between their proposals and reducing welfare dependency, but they did this in a way that would have further enlarged the loophole. They argued, for example, that those in the correctional system or in hospitals for the mentally ill were potentially recipients of public assistance (i.e., if released they might become recipients), and "if such groups are to be kept off the rolls, then preventive services must be begun at the stage before they enter the rolls." Expenditures on behalf of adult prison inmates were justified on the grounds that their incarceration was "responsible for family breakup which results in the family remaining outside needing to go on the AFDC [Aid to Families with Dependent Children] rolls."[6] This line of argument would have led the federal government far down the path of paying for state mental health programs and prisons, at a potential cost that would have been large indeed and way beyond the explicit intent of the 1967 amendments. Measured by operating expenditures, Mental Health was the biggest state agency in Illinois.

Besides enlarging the scope of purchased services and concentrating on state agencies, Illinois proposed a procedural breakthrough, complementary to its substantive proposals and highly important even if technical. It asked for a waiver of the single-state-agency requirement—several waivers, actually, one for each of the departments from which the Department of Public Aid would make purchases. (These included Children and Family Services and, eventually, Labor, as well as Mental Health and Corrections.) The Intergovernmental Cooperation Act of 1968 provided for waivers at the discretion of federal department heads. Because this law came after the initiation of California's preschool compensatory program, it could not have applied there, but by the time Illinois came along with its social service proposals in 1970, the secretary of HEW had granted several waivers, thus creating a precedent that Illinois could cite, although none of these earlier waivers, including one granted to Illinois itself, had applied to the use of social services funds. Here again, as with the purposes of expenditure, Illinois was profoundly challenging traditional public assistance administration. The single-state-agency requirement had been used by the Bureau of Family Services (BFS) to hold state welfare departments directly accountable for the use of federal grants. If the purposes of spending could be broadened and if the single-state-agency requirement could be bypassed, the states could easily turn services grants into a form of shared revenues, transferring federal public assistance funds to other state agencies more or less at will and using appropriations to other state agencies as matching funds in the federal public assistance program.

Alert, enterprising, and knowledgeable as the budget officials of Illinois certainly were, the inspiration for their bold proposals came largely from outsiders. They took cues from two sources primarily—Simpson, the SRS regional commissioner, and William Copeland, the consultant and professional promoter of services expenditures.

After becoming commissioner in 1969, Simpson had worked hard at starting child development programs in his region. He had urged Illinois and other states to do something about day care, and when the Illinois Department of Public Aid submitted a modest proposal late in September 1970 as an amendment to the state's social services plan, Simpson urged Swank to expand it. Simpson was particularly interested in setting up child-care centers in Chicago's public-housing projects, and he pointed out the possibilities of using services grants and model cities funds. For all this exhortation, which helped to galvanize state budget officials, Simpson's suggestions nevertheless remained within the bounds of the 1967 amendments and subsequent SRS regulations. They encouraged day care for poor and deprived children, and so did he. He was in touch with Jule Sugarman at HEW headquarters about this.

It was Copeland who, as one Illinois official outside the Budget Bureau said, really "expanded their minds." A magazine article by Copeland, fortuitously spotted by a budget staff member, brought the possibilities in services grants sharply to attention at a critical time. As a consequence, Illinois officials took a field trip to California and brought Copeland in for a briefing, which preceded their submission of plan amendments. Beginning in January, they employed him as a consultant. He turned out to be less helpful on the specifics of planning administration. A Budget Bureau examiner was assigned full time to that, and contracts worth nearly a million dollars were let to a major public accounting firm, Arthur Young and Company. Nevertheless, as one budget official later said, "We really do have to thank him. We would never have tried anything so outlandish except for him."

It became clear to Illinois officials after they made their proposals that HEW would not soon or lightly approve. Illinois had stepped into an area where rules were unclear and stakes were high. Technically, Simpson could have given approval. Under SRS rules, regional commissioners can approve state plan amendments but must refer disapproval to headquarters. Yet Simpson drew back once the plan was submitted, choosing instead to insist that officials in Washington decide. No neophyte, Simpson was a career federal official who had been assistant secretary of HEW for management in the Johnson administration. He fully recognized the national implications of the Illinois proposals. If national policy was in the making, he declared, it was up to officials in Washington to make it. Moreover, he was soon in a situation that limited his freedom to act in favor of the state. In February 1971 Governor Ogilvie announced that he was appointing Simpson director of public aid in Illinois to succeed Swank. The *Chicago Tribune* reported that Ogilvie expected Simpson to "be valuable in attempts to shift the entire welfare burden to the federal government."[7] The appointment eventually fell through, but while it was pending and to a degree afterward, Simpson as SRS commissioner felt constrained by the conflict of interest. For a while he ceased to sign correspondence to Illinois officials.

Of course, if Simpson had been more concerned to avoid committing the federal government, he could have discouraged Illinois from submitting the plan amendments in the first place. Once the plan had been formally transmitted to him with his informal acquiescence, HEW's choices began to narrow. It would be hard for the SRS to repudiate what its regional commissioner had received without objection—had even, in some respects, solicited. Some of the SRS regional staff in Chicago thought that it was precisely the national implications of the case that drew Simpson so deeply into it. He had operated in the national sphere before. As regional commissioner, that seemed still to be his inclination. As assistant secretary of HEW, he had collaborated with John Gardner, Wilbur Cohen, and Lisle Carter, assistant secretary for individual and family services, in planning the reorganization of 1967. Afterward he sought appointment as a regional commissioner of the SRS (though he did not expect anyone to believe that; it was generally supposed that the regional job was a haven secured for him by his friends in the department when the Republicans won the election). Consistent with the principles of the reorganization and with his own career as a managerial expert rather than a program specialist, he sought to assert leadership, to be the chief executive for the SRS in the region, and not to leave matters to the program specialists in the regional office.

Simpson had tried to take the lead in program development for child care and, more or less as the accidental consequence of that effort, found himself to be taking a lead on social services grants. He was on friendly terms with McCarter, whom he had known in Washington, and was drawn to the milieu of the Ogilvie administration—the bright young men, quick, progressive, doers. He had the air of a doer himself and, though a career bureaucrat, was overtly impatient with bureaucratic ways—the delays, the tedium, the hair-splitting phrases, the cautious evasions, the forms, the words, the paperwork to no seeming purpose. Public assistance administration in particular exasperated him. His manner was forceful, clear, and crisp, which made him effective in meetings. Later it would be said that he took the side of the state. But he was not an advocate for the state, he said. He was an advocate for clarity.

Simpson's demand for guidance brought no response from the SRS headquarters. (As time passed without action, he would promise Illinois and threaten the SRS that he would approve the plan himself if necessary—but he didn't.) Simpson saw the national implications; so did officials at the SRS headquarters. As he shrank from taking responsibility, so, with less justification, did they, and this reluctance deepened after the decision was taken and the magnitude of the costs became apparent. Following is the sworn testimony of James A. Bax, who replaced Stephen Simonds as commissioner of the Community Services Administration (CSA) in June 1971 and thus was the head of the responsible administrative unit of HEW when the Illinois plan was acted on:

Q. Who made the decision to approve the Illinois proposal?

A. I think the signature on the plans would be that of Don Simpson, who was the Regional Administrator or the Regional Commissioner of SRS, Region 5.

Q. That wasn't my question to you. If you know, who made the decision to approve the Illinois arrangement?

A. I presume it was a joint decision.

Q. Did you make it?

A. That decision was not mine to make.

Q. Would Mr. Twiname have made it?

A. I don't know if Mr. Twiname made it or someone else made that decision.

Q. Could it have been possibly Secretary Richardson, I believe he was the Secretary at that time, did he make that decision?

A. I have no knowledge of whether Simpson or Richardson did or not.

Q. What is your best knowledge as to who made that particular decision?

A. Again, I think there were many actors in the making of that decision and I have no direct knowledge and it would be hearsay if I were—there were some rumors how it was made and I have no direct knowledge of who made the decision that HEW would approve that state plan.[8]

Bax's testimony was not as evasive and disingenuous as it probably seems. The decision to approve the Illinois plan, like most important decisions in government, was not taken at one point by one identifiable official. It was the outcome of a complicated stream of events in which HEW's commitments evolved and choices narrowed as time passed. Approval came in three steps. The first was a memorandum issued to SRS regional commissioners on June 17, 1971, which set forth guidance on the purchase of services from public agencies. The policy stated in this memorandum was highly favorable to Illinois. The second came at the end of September 1971, when the SRS formally approved the plan submissions—that is, the responsible federal official, Simpson, signed them. The last came in February 1972, when HEW Secretary Elliot Richardson granted Illinois four waivers of the single-state-agency requirement.

At each of these three steps, Ogilvie's staff put as much pressure on the federal administration as they could. Assuming that Simpson had already done all he could for them, they concentrated on officials in Washington. Illinois had an office in Washington, which the Ogilvie administration had upgraded. Formerly part of an executive department and devoted to securing new industry, under Ogilvie it was made part of the governor's office, staffed with yet more bright young men, and charged to serve the full range of state interests in Washington. Lobbying for the Illinois plan amendments, however, was not left to this office alone. It received reinforcements from Springfield. Budget officials traveled to Washington repeatedly to press their case, and the governor himself was active. He too came to Washington, and got on the telephone to urge the Nixon administration to help. In repeated meetings with federal officials, Illinois officials advanced political, fiscal, and legal arguments, mixing these according to the audience. Politically, they argued their own weakness. Ogilvie was in danger of losing the 1972 election and might drag the President down with him in Illinois. They described their fiscal situation in dire terms and argued that their claims for services funds were within the law; HEW had no grounds for refusing. Finally, they cited the California precedent, insisting that they were entitled to equal treatment, an argument that

Tom Joe in particular was in no position to rebut.* By all accounts, they bargained very hard, and not just for services funds. Meetings were not confined to that subject; they were looking for any and all relief that they might find in HEW, with its vast and varied stock of federal benefits. During the first and crucial round of lobbying in the spring of 1971, Illinois met resistance from the Office of Management and Budget (OMB) and from career officials and program specialists in HEW. The Illinois officials' success came with appointive, policy-level officials in HEW—Tom Joe and John Twiname.

At first, Illinois officials concentrated on political appointees in the OMB. In May they stated their case to Assistant Director Richard P. Nathan. They "got no friendly counsel from Nathan," one of them recalled. Nathan asked skeptical questions about their fiscal situation and then repeated "the party line" that the Family Assistance Plan and revenue sharing would pass, obviating the state's need for other help. Next, Governor Ogilvie and McCarter saw Budget Director George Shultz, who happened to be from Illinois. He had been a professor at the University of Chicago. Shultz kept them waiting for forty minutes and then dominated the conversation, telling them that their estimates of gross national product were wrong—they would have more state revenue than they thought. They had no chance to state their case. McCarter thought it discourteous treatment of the governor of a major state.

Turned away by the OMB, Illinois officials proceeded to concentrate on the administering agency, the SRS. There too, the agency director, Twiname, was from Illinois. He was a friend of Donald Rumsfeld, a former congressman whom President Nixon had appointed director of the Office of Economic Opportunity and then a counselor to the President. "We were going with Twiname," an Illinois official later recalled of this

---

* In the eyes of Illinois officials, they were not doing anything that California had not done. Joe, however, would later insist that the cases were dissimilar— that California had used federal funds to expand programs, whereas Illinois was proposing in large part to substitute federal for state funds. That there was a sizable amount of substitution in Illinois seems clear. Whether the order of magnitude was significantly less in California would be hard to establish. In its first big use of the purchase technique, California did create a new program of preschool compensatory education for low-income children. In interviews, HEW officials who remarked on California's extreme acquisitiveness would often remark also on the superior use it made of federal funds.

period of the negotiations. "We nearly wore out our welcome with Twiname."

In meetings with Twiname's subordinates—the career officials in the Community Services Administration (CSA) who were technical and program specialists—Illinois officials could get no firm answers to anything. Even John Cotton, a phlegmatic man, lost his temper. It was like a *Catch-22* scene, he later said. Simpson too would remark on how very frustrating it was, trying to get the program people in the CSA to say something definite. Those veteran program specialists who remained in the central and regional offices after the general depletion of their ranks in the late 1960s appear to have had deep misgivings about the Illinois proposals. This was true specifically of those whose experience had been in the BFS. Yet they did not put up much resistance. On the whole, their misgivings were muted. To exert restraint they needed signs from policy-level, appointive officials that restraint was wanted. For some time, however, all the signs had pointed toward expansion.

Then, too, the role of program specialists was being deliberately reduced by reorganization. Within the developing organization of the SRS, Simpson's channel of communication to headquarters was a director of field operations, conceived as a generalist office. (The first incumbent was William J. Page, Jr., like Simpson a career official who thought of himself as a public administrator.) Within the regional office, Simpson did not rely heavily on the staff specialists in services; in the negotiations with Illinois, his principal assistant was the deputy commissioner in charge of relations with Illinois.

Finally, a sense that politics was involved—that is, the interest of a Republican administration in helping a Republican governor to retain his office—contributed to the caution of career officials. They knew, of course, what every school child knows—that Illinois is a big state—and what every beginning student of American government knows—that its electoral votes are very important in a presidential election. The bald facts of the case made it political. Beyond that, some in the SRS sensed that there had been signals from above—the White House, presumably. On their rounds of HEW, Illinois officials were cultivating the impression of highly placed political support. "If that impression was left, I'm glad," one later said. They would drop the fact that they had just come from the OMB, omitting to add, of course, that its director had rebuffed them. (The feeling in Illinois was quite the reverse of that in HEW.

Their anger rising, Ogilvie's staff believed that the President and his staff "weren't doing a goddamn thing for us," one recalled.) Within HEW, McCarter relied on old school ties to open doors, not on the intercession of the Nixon White House. In securing appointments, he had help from his friend Bob Patricelli, the deputy under secretary for policy, who had been a White House fellow the year before McCarter. Later, at the end of the summer, Governor Ogilvie would succeed in engaging the personal attention of the President, but in the spring he and his men were "going with Twiname."

Twiname's reaction was that he would like to do what he could within the bounds of law and regulations. Everyone should sit down and talk the matter over to see what that might be. As early as February, McCarter had seen Twiname in Washington in a meeting in the office of HEW Comptroller Bruce Cardwell, given him copies of the state's plan submissions to Simpson, and told him that the governor's budget was based on the assumption that HEW would approve.* Ogilvie himself pressed the state's case with Twiname, calling on him in Washington and making the appeal a very personal one, though their acquaintance had been casual, not close. Twiname felt constrained by his Illinois connection. Later he would recall that he had to bend over backward to avoid favoring his home state. Those who observed him at the time thought he was in a very difficult spot.

In the end it was Tom Joe who took matters in hand. With the assistance of Joel Cohen, HEW's assistant general counsel for the SRS, he drafted the memorandum of June 17, 1971, that gave regional offices guidance on the purchase of services from public agencies. Though cast in general terms, this memorandum was a response to the Illinois case. Indeed, according to Joe, it began as a position paper for Twiname's

---

* Twiname's reaction to this is revealed by the following memorandum, which he sent to Jack Costa, commissioner of the Assistance Payments Administration, on March 8, 1971: "The Governor's budget submission in Illinois is predicated on the fact that we are 99% of the way home in approving their plan amendment. A phone conversation with [a regional official in Chicago] last week confirmed that there were no hookers in the proposal, but that we were just ironing out final technical points. I want to make absolutely sure this is the case, and ask your help in expediting approval in the event Central Office is playing any part. I will assume there are no problems unless you tell me otherwise immediately. Note: I am attaching 2 letters addressed to Simpson which were given to me by the State Budget Director at his meeting here with Bruce Cardwell."

use in a forthcoming meeting with Illinois officials. Joe and Cohen put the first draft together in a matter of hours so that Twiname would not have to confront the Illinois delegation empty-handed. Before being issued, the memorandum was reviewed with Simpson, who suggested some changes in wording, and it was worked on by a few officials in the CSA, including the outgoing commissioner, Simonds, who signed it four days after Bax had replaced him.[9] Twiname approved it.

The June 17 memorandum repudiated the old BFS policy that purchase should not be used to pay for activities that are normally the responsibility of other state agencies. This new interpretation relied heavily on a phrase in the Social Security Act dating from 1956, which stipulates that state plans should describe services given to assistance recipients and the steps taken to assure "maximum utilization" of other agencies. This language, which was enacted before federal matching of purchase had been authorized, now was used to justify a very broad interpretation of the permissible scope of purchase. Citing "programmatic developments" as well as changes in the statute, the memorandum stated:

Purchase of services [from other public agencies] now provides a meaningful alternative to the furnishing of services directly by staff of the State or local agency.

The broad definitions of social services [following the 1962 and 1967 amendments] inevitably lead to inclusion of activities which have previously been considered the province only of other agencies. . . . The development of comprehensive services has combined what were formerly the interest of several agencies, and no agency can claim an exclusive franchise on the product. When such activities are carried out in the community, the State or local agency should properly assume its share of financial support, even though another agency actually provides the service. All the public agencies must be increasingly responsive to the needs of the poor and the community as a whole. . . .

In this context, "maximum utilization" of other agencies . . . must be construed flexibly and realistically in the light of today's situation.[10]

A policy that federal public assistance funds should not pay for activities that are normally the responsibility of other state agencies had finally been turned upside down. They *should* be so used, when public services are being offered to poor people. This was what Joe had said in his paper for the American Public Welfare Association in 1968 and what he had been saying to state and local officials, but it had not

emerged as explicit SRS policy before June 17.* Only two broad kinds
of state social services were excluded. One was public education. The
memorandum said it would not be appropriate to use federal social services funds to pay for the regular school costs of public assistance recipients. It said also that institutional care of the mentally ill remained
entirely a state and local responsibility. However, that did not rule out
financing new or additional social services in public schools or mental
hospitals. Some sources in the SRS recalled that in preceding months
Joe had indicated a wish to go further with federal support of institutional care, and they surmised that at this point Cohen drew a line.
There was a history of contrary action by Congress. The memorandum
pointed out that Congress had repeatedly declined to provide public
assistance funds for mental, correctional, or children's institutions.

Joe, it is safe to say, could be confident that the policy he stated was
one that Under Secretary Veneman approved, though neither man recalls that Veneman did approve the actual document. "If I didn't clear
it," Veneman later said, "Tom did it with the assumption that I *would*
approve"—and that was "a fair assumption." Veneman explained that
"Tom knew pretty much where I was on this, we talked so often."
Veneman talked often, too, with governors who were interested in
services grants; by all accounts, he was keenly sensitive to the political
elements of grant-in-aid administration. He favored making federal services grants available for broad purposes (as long, so he later said, as they
were used to expand state programs), and within the department his
views were likely to be conclusive, for Secretary Richardson left welfare
very much to him unless major new legislation was involved. Social
security, social services, Medicare, Medicaid—all these were "principally
Veneman's bag," an aide to Richardson recalled.

Cohen, as a career civil servant and lawyer with long experience of

* The steps in this evolution were from explicit prohibition (1962) to silence
(1969) to an explicit statement of obligation. The 1969 SRS regulations sanctioned
a wide-ranging use of funds. The preliminary version appearing in the *Federal
Register* in July 1968 said that the SRS "encourages States to view Title IV-A as the
vehicle for providing a full range of services to those families needing services who are
on AFDC rolls as well as necessary services to families who have been or are likely
to become eligible for AFDC." (Vol. 33, no. 138, July 17, 1968, p. 10235.) But
even this language, encouraging as it was in regard to purchases on behalf of eligible
families, stopped short of saying that the public assistance program ought, through
purchase, to pick up some share of the cost of activities hitherto the responsibility
of other public agencies.

public assistance administration, might have been expected to insist on a tighter document. Illinois officials had found him to be extremely tough—he was the "villain," according to an Illinois source, "a formidable opponent." In meetings, the program specialists had seemed to defer to him, and he had been able to pose objections that had the Illinois contingent worried. This was so despite the fact that he was busy and burdened with issues of more urgency, among which were a series of contests with California and other states over the enforcement of federal welfare laws.[11] All in all, it was a very demanding time. Cohen, however, besides conducting the defense episodically in a small fraction of his time, was conducting it with a weak law, and Illinois put him on notice that it would exploit the legal weakness. In late May, after a hard session with him, Illinois officials went straight from HEW to Covington and Burling—"the best law firm in town," an Illinois man said—and hired a lawyer to prepare a brief supporting their claims, "to convey to Cohen that we were serious."[12] (Illinois paid 75 percent of the fee with federal funds.)

Cohen deferred to political leadership; both he and Joe understood that Joe would be responsible for the contents of the June 17 memorandum. Typically, an HEW lawyer eschews "making policy" but advises the appointive agency head whether the policy he proposes is proscribed by law; he identifies the range of the policymaker's discretion. In this case, the proscriptions of the law were few, the range of permissible discretion was enormous, and the social context of policymaking had changed a great deal in a short time. Therefore Cohen as assistant general counsel could with a perfectly clear conscience sign off on policies in 1969 or 1971 that were very different from those of a few years before. That he had so active a part in preparing this particular memorandum, a document not much distinguished by a lawyer's precision, is itself anomalous and is partly to be accounted for by the default in the SRS, which for some time had been trying unsuccessfully to come up with new policies on social services. Twiname did not seize the issues posed by Illinois, and the CSA was immobilized by a lack of both leadership and experienced staff, as well as by the air of high politics that hung over the case. Joe, who disdained bureaucratic channels and who had made social services his business for some time, stepped in or was drawn in and then drew Cohen in too—informally, as Cohen thought of it, rather than officially as assistant general counsel.

Impressed into service at Joe's request and mindful of Joe's blindness, which required working in tandem on such matters, Cohen became on the spur of the moment the drafter of a policy document rather than a lawyer independently advising his client, although he reserved the right to raise legal questions. The draft that he wrote mixed Joe's language with what Cohen understood to be Twiname's policy preferences and what he presumed to be codification of actual administrative practice.

The authors of the June 17 memorandum did not regard it as a wholesale concession. In truth, no one at headquarters knew just how much of a concession it might be, because no one there knew precisely what the regional offices had been approving for inclusion in state plans. Illinois officials, on the other hand, seemed to know, and made clear that they expected approval for anything anyone else had done or planned to do. The memorandum did mix constraints with the concessions, and the mix could vary from state to state. What Illinois saw as constraint could for some other state define a vast range of fresh possibility. In the context of the Illinois demands, the memorandum seemed a compromise and an instance of drawing lines where none had been drawn before. Besides drawing the line at certain types of expenditures desired by the state (Illinois, after all, was much interested in matching institutional expenses, and in negotiations it had begun to advance claims for education), the memorandum reasserted the single-state-agency principle: the state public assistance agency "must remain as the point of responsibility for all activities under the program," including determinations of individual eligibility and the provision of purchased services. The memorandum applied only to situations in which the state agency purchased services with funds directly appropriated; it explicitly declined to discuss the use of state funds, other than public assistance appropriations, as the state matching share of services costs. Noting that federal regulations required an agreement between the state public assistance agency and the service provider, the memorandum stipulated that "Federal matching in costs is available only from the point at which the agreement is in effect and services under it are delivered to eligible clientele." These provisions could have constituted defenses against the Illinois claims had policy-level officials been determined on defense. Finally, the memorandum provided that federal funds should not be used "merely to replace State and local funds." They should "result in a significantly expanded amount of public services for poor people," a provision that Joe would later insist was the crux of the memorandum and a significant new assertion of federal control. Cohen wanted to require expansion of service in strict proportion to the increase of federal funds, but Joe thought that was too harsh.

In all, this memorandum was an extraordinary public document. In content, it was high policy. Basic principles of public assistance administration and possibly hundreds of millions of dollars in federal funds were at stake.[13] In form, however, it was treated as less than policy. This was a memorandum of "clarification," not a regulation; thus Twiname's office did not put it through the elaborate process of review and clearance that is used for regulations. It was not cleared with the HEW comptroller or with the secretary. It was not addressed to state governments but to federal regional officials "as a basis for negotiations with State agencies and evaluation of State plans." And it was signed by a man who had ceased to hold office.

Naturally, SRS regional officials were puzzled by this document and asked guidance on what to do with it. The reply from headquarters in July surpassed the original in equivocation. A memorandum from Commissioner Bax explained that state officials were generally aware of the contents, since Twiname had discussed the June 17 memorandum at a meeting of the Council of State Public Welfare Administrators, but that headquarters did not "intend to publish the statement or issue it formally to State agencies at this time . . . it is a flexible document, subject to such change as may prove to be necessary." Bax then proceeded to add: "I urge you to share the content of this statement with the States. However, if you distribute copies of the actual statement, they should be clearly marked DRAFT." Draft or not, the regional offices were instructed to use the memorandum as "guidance material" in assisting the states in program development.[14]

Alone among the principals, Cohen appears to have doubted whether this document should be distributed at all. Besides being highly irregular in form, it ran the risk of stimulating demand. On the other hand, Cohen shared with Joe and Twiname a concern that the SRS should issue something. Illinois and other states were opening up new questions, discrepancies among states and federal administrative regions were growing, and the SRS needed to interpret the regulations, which were proving inadequate. Moreover, it was hard to argue that if this were guidance for the case of Illinois, it should not be guidance in other cases too. If the memorandum did stimulate demand, both Joe and Twiname were wholly willing to accept that result, although they did not foresee quite the explosion that was to occur. For the issuance to be informal and to be signed by the outgoing, relatively low-ranking Simonds was thought to minimize the risks; if necessary, the SRS could recant, whereas regulations would have been nearly immutable. Regulations would also have taken a long time to prepare, and Illinois was impatient.

For his part, Simonds thought that clarification of SRS policy and further encouragement to the states were desirable. He had been contemplating some such initiative himself, he later said. In his recollection, and his alone, his office played a large part in drafting the document. He did not think of the memorandum as a response to any particular state, and, indeed, he appears to have been unaware of the intense pressures from Illinois, which were directed at higher offices than his.

Equivocal as it was—or as its sponsors wished it to be—the memorandum made crucial concessions to Illinois. Though they professed disappointment at the time, Illinois officials were "very gratified," as one later acknowledged. After June 17, it would have been difficult for HEW to reject the Illinois plan proposals. Yet approvals did not immediately follow. Ostensibly a clarification, the memorandum still left much to interpretation, especially as to whether federal funds would supplant state funds. Negotiations went on.

As the end of September approached, Illinois pressed for a decision. The SRS could not delay forever, and September 30 was a deadline in the eyes of state officials who believed that Illinois would lose the right to certain retroactive federal reimbursement if approval were not received before the start of the second quarter of fiscal year 1972 on October 1, 1971. As that date approached, Illinois secured a meeting in Washington with Twiname.

At this session, which took place on September 27, there was one last round of negotiation. Illinois officials put forth their proposals. Simpson raised questions, which Illinois answered. (This much was rehearsed, some at the meeting concluded, and Tom Joe angrily reported in a memorandum to Under Secretary Veneman that Simpson had taken the side of the state.) Twiname did not have much to say. As usual, it was Joel Cohen who put the hard questions. To the surprise and disappointment of the Illinois delegation, Joe was also challenging and critical. Because he had been encouraging before, they had regarded him as an ally.* Since when had he turned so restrictive, someone from Illinois wanted to know. There was an exchange of remarks about refinancing—whether Illinois was doing it, followed by insinuations from the Illinois side about where they had learned how to do it. The meeting did not resolve all the issues, and at least one participant, a member of the HEW comptroller's office who was a newcomer to the deliberations over Illinois, did not realize that anything had been decided. For a while thereafter, he went around asking others in the department what had happened to the Illinois plan. He did not know that immediately afterward, Simpson, with Twiname's approval, had signed it, and that the SRS had approved interagency agreements covering the purchase of service by the Illinois Department of Public Aid from the departments of Mental Health and Corrections.†

It is possible that John D. Ehrlichman, the President's domestic counselor, interceded in the Illinois case at this point. In mid-August, Governor Ogilvie had a chance to explain his plight personally to President Nixon when the President visited the Illinois state fair in Springfield. The two were together in a limousine for perhaps half an hour. Again, more briefly, Ogilvie saw Nixon on September 3, when the President was in Chicago to address the annual convention of the Associated Milk Producers, Inc. The President responded sympathetically to Ogilvie's account of his fiscal and political problems, and referred the governor to Ehrlichman. There is circumstantial evidence that after Illinois had secured the September 27 meeting with Twiname but before the meeting took place, Governor Ogilvie called Ehrlichman to appeal

* Some months before their initiative in the fall of 1970, Illinois officials had heard Joe explain the potentialities in services grants and, ironically, they had failed to respond. The occasion was a meeting in Washington arranged by members of HEW's Center for Community Planning, who were soliciting the cooperation of Illinois officials in support of the model cities program in Chicago. These HEW officials wanted an Illinois delegation to hear Joe on the subject of federal funding. In the context of an appeal from federal officials to help Chicago's model cities program, members of the governor's office did not prove much interested in social services grants, but when they had their own budget deficit to consider, they recalled the advice received on this occasion and proceeded to use it in a way that Joe probably did not anticipate. Joe would insist later that he had never encouraged the states to engage in refinancing; other sources, including an Illinois official, claimed that he did.

† Approval of the agreement with the Department of Children and Family Services, much the easiest case, had come in July.

for his intervention. Ogilvie recalls having made such a call; Ehrlichman does not recall having received it. Veneman recalls receiving instructions from the White House, either directly or via the secretary's office, to "do what you can for Illinois," probably on this occasion, though he could not pinpoint the date. Twiname, asked if there had been a political decision higher in the administration to approve the plan, could not recall any pressure from above. He added that he approved the plan in September without reluctance. He had no reason not to approve it, he said. With or without political intervention by the White House at this point, there seems to have been a feeling among both Illinois and SRS officials that they had done all the negotiating they were going to do, and that a point of decision had been reached.

Yet this was not the final decision. The climactic confrontation between Illinois and the Nixon administration was still to come. Ordinarily, plan approvals would have disposed of the case, but this was not an ordinary case. HEW still had to grant single-state-agency waivers. The governor's staff therefore was not sure just what obstacles lay ahead, or just how much Illinois could realize from services grants and when. They would not be satisfied until they actually saw the money, for which they were daily more desperate. Neither the Family Assistance Plan nor revenue sharing, on which the Ogilvie administration also had been counting, had passed, and in August, as part of a "new economic policy," the President had announced that they were to be postponed. But there was no halt in the rise of welfare costs. In the fall of 1971 Ogilvie's budget office was estimating the state's welfare deficit for fiscal year 1972 at $107 million. By counting on federal funds to make this up, the Ogilvie administration had sacrificed other alternatives. Borrowing or shifting funds around among state accounts would have required legislative approval, which could not be obtained. The legislature would have insisted on cutting welfare grants. And it was now too late even for that. Had it been done a year or two earlier when a deficit in the welfare budget had first been anticipated, sizable savings might have been realized from small and relatively acceptable cuts, on the order of 5 percent. To make up the deficit at this late point, however, would have required cuts on the order of 20 percent, which was simply unthinkable. In this situation, Illinois opened action on new fronts.

In Springfield, the governor moved to cut welfare costs in a highly selective way. Early in October he announced changes in the Medicaid program that were estimated to save $50 million. He also announced a plan to cut back on general assistance, the relief program for persons ineligible for the federally aided categories (AFDC, and aid to the aged, blind, and disabled). He proposed to transfer $21 million from general assistance to AFDC, where the money would be matched with federal funds. The governor's staff believed that many people on general assistance in Cook County, which receives more than 90 percent of the state's general assistance expenditures, were actually eligible for the federally aided categories but were on general assistance because the Cook County Department of Public Aid did not want to cope with the paperwork.[15]

In Washington, the state prepared to take legislative action. The Illinois office in Washington had conceived the idea of emergency federal legislation to relieve the states of increases in welfare costs for a year beginning on June 30, 1971. That is, the states would be "held harmless" against the rise in welfare costs. This relief would be offered only to states that had not tightened eligibility standards or lowered standards of cash payment in the categorical programs, which of course included Illinois. Governor Ogilvie had broached this idea to President Nixon in August, hinting that California and New York might also be interested, and at the President's invitation he had submitted a proposal to Ehrlichman. The administration did not agree to it, however. Budget Director Shultz was thoroughly opposed to the idea, which would have added a billion dollars to the federal budget and set a bad precedent in intergovernmental fiscal relations. Secretary Richardson and other proponents of the Family Assistance Plan within the administration feared as well that the proposal would deprive states of an incentive to support welfare reform. In an interview with a reporter from the *Chicago Tribune*, Richardson said he could not foresee administration support for the proposal. The interview appeared in the *Tribune* on November 3—the very day, as it happened, on which Illinois newspapers also reported a decision by the state supreme court against Governor Ogilvie's plan to cut general assistance. A suit by Cook County, successful in a state circuit court, had been upheld.[16] The governor's situation seemed steadily to be growing worse.

Success, however, was not far off for Illinois. Fortuitously, the attempt to cut welfare at home made it possible to achieve victory in Washington, for it drew the state's senior senator, liberal Republican Charles H. Percy, into the contest on Ogilvie's side. After Ogilvie announced the cuts, a nationally known black leader from Chicago, Jesse Jackson—the director of a poor-people's movement called Operation Breadbasket— came to Washington to appeal to Senator Percy to intercede with Ogilvie.* After consulting with Ogilvie's Washington office, Percy responded by promising active support for hold-harmless legislation for the states. He thereupon set out to gather support for the proposal from governors and other senators. He announced that he would introduce the bill if it had administration support.

As it happened, Illinois did not wait for the President and his staff to acquiesce in the bill. It took advantage of the administration's opposition.

On November 15, Senator Percy introduced the hold-harmless proposal as an amendment to the President's tax reduction bill, part of a package of economic legislation to which the administration attached highest priority. In November, it appeared to be the only major legislation likely to be acted upon before the end of the year; it was, an Illinois official said, "the last car going." Hence Illinois got on board with the Percy amendment, in a last-ditch effort to extract concessions from the Nixon administration. Opposed to the Percy amendment as such, the administration also wanted to prevent extraneous amendments to the tax bill, especially if they related to social security or welfare, subjects that would have opened up an interminable debate. Accordingly, no sooner had the Percy amendment been introduced than the administration offered to pay to remove it. "We got their attention, didn't we?" an Illinois man later observed of this moment.

On November 16, Percy and Thomas J. Corcoran, the head of the Illinois office in Washington, met with Ehrlichman; Paul H. O'Neill, who had succeeded Nathan as assistant director of the OMB; and a man from Vice-President Spiro T. Agnew's office who handled relations with the states. The meeting was held in the vice-president's office in the Senate. Governor Ogilvie was to have been there but at the last minute did not come, having been detained by state business and deterred by the advice of his Washington staff. Corcoran, who had written

* In a speech to the members of Operation Breadbasket in October, Percy said of Jackson, according to the *Chicago Tribune*: "Jesse knows how to move politics and get things done. If the President of the United States Steel Corporation calls me while I am on the Senate floor, I tell my secretary to tell him I will call him back. But when Jesse Jackson calls, I tell her to tell him I will be with him as soon as I can get off the [Senate] floor." (October 24, 1971.)

a master's thesis on Woodrow Wilson, remembered the lesson that Wilson should not have gone to Versailles. He was relieved when Ogilvie did not come to the meeting with Ehrlichman. Ehrlichman appealed to Percy and to Corcoran as the governor's representative to support the President's program. Illinois had reached a fork in the road, he said, describing the choice with his hands. (Illinois officials would later recall the phrase with high indignation.) It would either take the path of helping a Republican President achieve his purposes or it would pursue a selfish, obstructionist course: Illinois should decide which way it wanted to go.

Illinois was told that if Percy would withdraw his amendment, the administration would make several concessions, among them that HEW would complete action on the state's social services proposals. Other items included backing for some of the cost-cutting measures that the governor had announced. For example, the OMB estimated that the state could save $20 million to $30 million by transferring eligible people from general assistance to the categories, and the federal administration would accede to a claim for retroactive reimbursement in such cases, which O'Neill suggested would yield around $5 million. He also proposed that the federal administration advance the state's public assistance grant for the first quarter of fiscal year 1973. Amounting to about $50 million, that grant, if made in the last quarter of fiscal year 1972, would go a long way toward making up the state's deficit. Percy countered that Ogilvie would have to assure him that the offer was acceptable and that he needed to cover his own commitment to other senators and to governors whose support he had enlisted for the amendment. Twenty governors were supporting him. That night, a delegation from the Illinois Budget Bureau flew to Washington to represent the governor in negotiations.

On November 17, the Illinois group met with O'Neill. They reviewed what the federal government might do for Illinois. As would any man in his place, O'Neill was casting about for items of expenditure that could be given legally and at low cost. Sensing a strong bargaining position, for the administration thought the Percy amendment had a good chance to pass, Illinois was lengthening its list of demands, which now ran to fifteen or sixteen items. The discussion ranged over water resources, health, and food stamps as well as welfare. Not much was said of social services, which were mutually understood to be part of the package. In particular, it is not clear that there was a shared understanding of what the Illinois social services proposals would cost. In the spring, Illinois officials had $75 million in mind. In November they seem to have been anticipating a greater yield but not to have revealed the precise magnitude of their aspirations to O'Neill. The open-endedness of the law and the uncertainty of federal laws and regulations left that figure in doubt. At the end, Illinois officials said they were not satisfied with O'Neill's offer. It was not enough to induce them to agree to withdrawing the Percy amendment. They then left for Capitol Hill, where debate on the amendment was starting.

In mid-debate, Percy got a better offer from Ehrlichman—better, not in what it contained regarding social services, which was being treated as a settled item, but in its response to the substance of the Percy amendment. Ehrlichman agreed. that the amendment could be incorporated in the administration's welfare reform bill. In debate, Percy then elicited a pledge from Senator Russell B. Long, chairman of the Finance Committee, that the welfare bill would be reported by March 1 and pledges from Long and Senator Abraham Ribicoff, who would be a key figure in the welfare debate, not to oppose his amendment.[17] O'Neill, according to Illinois sources, was very upset over Ehrlichman's concession, which Ehrlichman later defended by saying that he had avoided a present danger for a speculative one. Within the administration, the proponents of the Family Assistance Plan had come to regard the Percy amendment as an asset when linked to welfare reform, for it would increase the incentive to the states to support legislation.[18] George Shultz continued to be deeply opposed, and personally called Ogilvie in a vain effort to reverse the outcome.

Ultimately, neither the Family Assistance Plan nor the Percy amendment passed, but social services grants were soon well on their way to providing the billion dollars in federal fiscal relief that the amendment would have provided. It is unlikely that either Ehrlichman or O'Neill anticipated this. In the November confrontation, social services grants were just one chip among many with which they tried to buy off Illinois in order to avoid the billion dollar cost and the bad precedents embodied in the Percy amendment.*

* Lacking access to OMB or White House files, I have not been able to reconstruct to my own satisfaction just how the President's staff perceived this encounter with Illinois or precisely how they assessed the value of what they conceded, and

Presidential support proved helpful to Illinois in the last stages of its negotiations with HEW. In the spring Illinois officials could only hope to leave an impression that they had backing from the President's office. After November 17 they had the real thing.

For a while the question of whether Illinois should be granted waivers of the single-state-agency requirement moved through bureaucratic channels. Governor Ogilvie submitted two requests to Secretary Richardson on September 28 and two more on October 20. Within HEW they were referred to the Office of Field Operations (OFO) in the SRS and from there to interested program units—the Assistance Payments Administration, Medical Services Administration (MSA), and Community Services Administration. In November and December, all three agencies raised major questions about the waivers and recommended against approval. Unpredictably, the reaction from the CSA was particularly trenchant. CSA officials said that, judging from the justification submitted by the SRS regional office, Illinois was seeking the waivers in order to capture additional federal funds, a purpose for which federal law did not authorize waivers. Waivers, the CSA said rather starchily, were supposed to improve program administration.[19] The MSA was worried about the possible effects of the Illinois proposals on its own program costs, as the following memorandum indicates:

---

recollections for the record are far less available and acute in Washington than in Chicago and Springfield. My account is derived almost wholly from Illinois sources. O'Neill, at least, was surely aware that major concessions to Illinois would make services grants much harder to control elsewhere. I doubt, however, that he knew or could have known exactly how much that particular concession would finally cost in Illinois, let alone as a precedent for other states. Nor is it likely that he and Ehrlichman knew that as a precedent, the Illinois case had indirectly been working its effects for several months, ever since the June 17 memorandum appeared. In the fall of 1971, the OMB was just beginning to sense that an explosion was in the making, and it was more worried about New York than about Illinois. In their lobbying with the President's staff, Illinois officials minimized the fiscal implications of their request. A briefing paper that the budget staff prepared for Governor Ogilvie in late September contains the following statement for the governor's use in a prospective phone conversation with Ehrlichman: "There is concern in HEW on the fiscal impact nationally. For Illinois we are talking a $15–20 million issue. It is extremely unlikely that many States will be able to react this year to have any significant fiscal [impact] on the federal budget, and 1973 or 1974 actions will have markedly different impact due to welfare reform or limitations such as the 110% the administration proposed this year." It is not clear where the $15–20 million figure came from. It was an understatement at the time, and grossly misleading as events turned out.

Through discussions with staff of OFO, APA, and CSA we have learned that the acceptability of an Illinois proposal for the purchase of services has a history of negotiations between Central Office, Regional Office and the State extending back at least to April 1971, in which MSA has not been a participant. A review of such records as have been made available to us revealed little or no discussion regarding the extent to which medical care would be purchased under the service programs with claiming of Federal financial participation at the 75% rate. In view of the potential impact of such a practice on program costs, we feel the need for clarification. . . .[20]

Simpson advised Illinois officials that proceeding through bureaucratic channels was hopeless and that they should again "use brass."

On February 1, 1972, Governor Ogilvie and Tom Corcoran called on Secretary Richardson to argue for the waivers and to urge that they be granted retroactively from the date on which plan amendments had become effective (October 1970). Richardson agreed. Behind the scenes, Illinois officials were claiming that the waivers were integral to the state's social services proposals, which Ehrlichman and O'Neill had agreed in November to approve, and they were insisting that O'Neill deliver on the commitment made then. An honorable man, he did. However, even had the November bargain never been struck, it would have been hard for Richardson to deny the waivers in view of Simpson's having encouraged Illinois many months before to use that technique. At Simpson's suggestion, the need for waivers had been noted in the original plan submission.

After Ogilvie's meeting with Richardson, Joel Cohen was asked to prepare an opinion on whether waivers could be granted retroactively. He found that the Intergovernmental Cooperation Act, an OMB circular on single-state-agency waivers, and departmental policies were silent on the question of effective date. But he also had to deal with the June 17 memo, in which he had himself included an explicit defense against the precise demand that Illinois was now making. Under great pressure, the administration had bargained that defense away, and he wrote:

We shall not attempt here to construe the effect of this issuance generally in relation to section 204 of the Intergovernmental Cooperation Act. Its application to Illinois can perhaps be decided separately. If, on the basis of the course of dealing between SRS and Illinois regarding the State plan amendments on purchase of social services, it can be determined that both before and after the June 17, 1971 issuance the State had reason to expect that waivers could be requested from the Secretary at a later date and granted without adverse effect on Federal funding of Illinois expenditures from the effective date of the plan amendments, then it would not be unreasonable, in our view, for SRS to treat the sentence in the June 17, 1971 issuance—whatever its effect in other situations—as not applicable to the negotiations with Illinois which were already in progress.[21]

Once again, federal policy was being shaped to meet the needs of the governor of Illinois.

Looking back on the spending explosion, many HEW officials blamed it on the President and his staff, who, they hinted, had played politics with social services. Bax, when pressed to answer who had approved the Illinois plan amendments, finally said that the OMB had done it. He testified:

I believe it would be my opinion that that decision was recognized by many people as setting a precedent and it was a very significant budgetary —a significant budget impact was made by—either made by or approved by someone in the Office of Management and Budget. I think OMB was the principal funding agency that made that decision. . . .[22]

The President's men did take some important last steps, but only after the department had taken the federal government very far down the path.

As planned, Illinois made up its budget deficit with federal funds. Ogilvie announced on February 15 that the state would receive $102 million in new social services grants in fiscal year 1972, more than the $75 million it had begun by counting on. Actually, Illinois ultimately received $188 million for fiscal year 1972, as well as an addition of $18.5 million to the $24.9 million that it had been granted in 1971. Thus its 1972 grant was $163.5 million more than the unadjusted 1971 grant, a very large increase. Illinois also received $60 million as an advance on its public assistance grant for the first quarter of 1973, although in this it got no special treatment in the end. The OMB concluded that it would be in the federal interest to make an advance payment to all states, in the amount of $1 billion. This cost the federal government nothing, enabled it to spread welfare expenditures more evenly over the two fiscal years, and helped to balance the budget announced in January 1972.[23] To the extent that this helped Illinois, it was "serendipitous," O'Neill later said, and Illinois officials agreed.

Governor Ogilvie lost the 1972 election. Reflecting soon thereafter on his four years in office, he identified the welfare crisis of 1971 as "the climactic issue," which he had dealt with by cutting general assistance costs and getting "large federal commitments on several fronts."[24] His budget staff, too, took satisfaction in the outcome. Deputy Director Cotton remarked on how experience had changed his perspective on budgeting. He had come to Illinois to introduce the latest analytic procedures but had found budgeting to be much more political than he had imagined. He concluded that the Budget Bureau "serves the Governor rather than some abstract notion of a budget system."[25] As a leading example of how the bureau had served the governor, he cited its success in securing federal public assistance funds.

While there was pride and satisfaction in Illinois, there was neither in HEW. The department's policy on social services was a shambles, and spending was out of control altogether.

CHAPTER EIGHT

Rising State Claims
and a Congressional Response

THE JUNE 17 MEMORANDUM advertised the potential for federal funding of social services. Though addressed to regional commissioners of the Social and Rehabilitation Service (SRS), it circulated instantly among the states. The American Public Welfare Association mimeographed and distributed it. In the Chicago region, Donald Simpson assembled all the state welfare directors and explained it to them. Almost daily thereafter, he talked on the phone with his counterpart in New York, Elmer W. Smith, about how to apply the new policy in their respective regions. Told how far they might go, states that formerly had held back advanced new claims.

Their claims were broad, consistent with the memorandum. When state and federal regional officials were told later that SRS headquarters regarded the memorandum as restrictive, they were incredulous. The director of social services in California, subsequently an official of the Department of Health, Education, and Welfare (HEW), recalled that on seeing the document for the first time he had exclaimed to his department director: "Tomorrow the world!" In the field, the memorandum was received as the sweeping liberalization of federal policy that in truth it was.[1]

Whatever expansive effect the document itself had was powerfully reinforced by the personality of James Bax, whose tenure as commissioner of the Community Services Administration (CSA) began just when the memo appeared. Stephen Simonds had been no man to bring spending under control, but whereas he was soft-spoken and professional, Bax was flamboyant and political. A Republican, he was recruited by John Twiname from the administration of Governor Claude

R. Kirk, Jr., of Florida, where he had succeeded in consolidating a number of hitherto separate and specialized social service agencies. (That was the kind of accomplishment that favorably impressed the Richardson administration at HEW, and it was also a technique by which states could facilitate the receipt and broadened use of federal services funds.) Whereas Simonds had seemed inhibited by being a Democratic holdover in a Republican administration, Bax was not inhibited by anything. He promptly began to promote social services spending by the states. The Bax philosophy, according to an aphorism that spread in HEW, was: "You hatch it, we match it." One of his memorandums is illustrative. The occasion was the failure, in August 1971, of an attempt by the Office of Management and Budget and the HEW comptroller to close the end on services spending by revising the appropriations act. Far from deferring to the President's wish for control, as expressed in the annual budget message, Bax turned the failure into an occasion for further expansion. He wrote to regional commissioners for community services:

Both the House and Senate have rejected the proposal in the 1972 budget to close the end on the appropriation. This should be good news for those States with a desire to expand worthwhile services. In fact, States might well consider the advantage inherent in building a comprehensive services base this year.[2]

Foremost among the post-June wave of new claimants was New York, last of the "big three" states to be heard from. California, Illinois, and New York together accounted for close to a third of the nation's welfare case load, and they were big politically too. They accounted in 1972 for more than a fifth of the 538 electoral votes, and all had Republican governors. Like Illinois—indeed like most of the states that took advantage of services funds—New York acted on the initiative of budget officials in the governor's office, not on that of the welfare commissioner. Only a year before, New York's welfare commissioner had turned down an appeal from New York City to exploit federal services funds. (In the city, the initiative came from the budget director, Frederick O'R. Hayes, and from a new director of human resources, Jule Sugarman, who knew better than anyone what opportunities lay in the federal regulations.) As with Illinois, the governor himself brought pressure to bear on the White House and the secretary of HEW. At one point, Nelson Rockefeller also sought the intercession of Attorney

General John N. Mitchell. Like Illinois, New York proposed massive purchases by the welfare department from other state agencies, but in New York the array was much wider: health, mental hygiene, education, correction, commerce, the narcotics addiction control commission, the division of youth, the office of aging, the division of probation, and the state university.[3] Illinois budget officials were angry when they learned that New York had brought in education.

Between them, New York and Illinois accounted for 70 percent of the near-billion dollar increase in services grants between fiscal years 1971 and 1972.[4] They largely account too for the fact that most of the increase came from purchases. Touche Ross and Company, an accounting firm hired by the CSA to find out where the money was going, reported early in 1973 that 80 percent of the increase between 1971 and 1972 was caused by an almost fourfold rise in purchased services and that over three-fourths of this was due to the jump in services purchased from other public agencies, mainly state departments of education, mental health and retardation, corrections, and narcotics and alcoholism control. Purchase from public agencies increased seventeen times over the level of fiscal year 1971. Touche Ross reported that "most of these services had been provided as state funded and operated programs prior to their 'purchase' by the public welfare agency. We found little evidence to conclude that the purchased services represented increased services or new service programs."[5] Clearly, federal services funds were being used by the states for fiscal relief.

Federal spending would have to be brought under control. The only question was who would do it in the election year of 1972. Who, as Secretary Richardson wryly put it in a press conference, would kill the goose that had laid the golden egg? Richardson's department wanted the President to do it. The President wanted the Congress to do it. Within Congress, the appropriations committees preferred that the authorizing committees do it. And the authorizing committees did, but only because they had other golden eggs to give.

Late in the fall of 1971 the CSA began a crash effort to prepare new regulations. Five task forces were assembled to consider various aspects of services administration, and Booz, Allen and Hamilton was engaged to give advice. (Booz, Allen designed and depicted a scheme that it called GOSS, a Goal-Oriented Social Service model, and that others called, a bit derisively, "Bax's boxes.") In testimony on the budget in

the spring of 1972, SRS officials promised Congress that the new guide-
lines would bring the program under control.[6] But when the HEW
comptroller's office saw what the CSA proposed to issue, it concluded that
the effect would be just the reverse. Much in the CSA scheme had no
meaning—the comptroller's staff thought Bax's boxes were empty, and
that insofar as meaning could be found, it would produce expansion. In
a memorandum to Secretary Richardson, the office warned that the
proposed regulations were "extremely dangerous." With a few excep-
tions, they would "perpetuate, and in some instances, accelerate the
uncontrolled increase in federal financing of services; further confuse the
already chaotic financing of services; create new mandatory services that
would commit—without discussion or analysis—hundreds of millions of
dollars in federal and state resources; defeat our goal of obtaining
rudimentary program and cost data on a systematic basis by mandating
such an elaborate structure that the states could not possibly cope with
it." The comptroller's office recommended eliminating every new or
expanded service, and prohibiting the use of services grants under the
public assistance titles for vocational rehabilitation, medical, health,
and mental health services except for family planning, and all residential care and subsistence. The memorandum acknowledged that factors other than cost would have to be taken into account. The comptroller's office would leave it to others to weigh those factors, but
concluded that "this is one time . . . that we feel that the weight of
both program and financial evidence is on the side of fiscal sanity."[7]

Faced with a stalemate between the SRS, which was backing the new
regulations, and the comptroller's office, which was opposing them, the
secretary's office in HEW elected to let the President decide, which was
a prudent course anyway in view of the history of White House involvement and the political sensitivity of the matter. On June 23, which was
a Friday, Secretary Richardson sent the President a memorandum out-
lining a choice of administrative actions and stating that a decision by
early the next week was "imperative."

As Secretary Richardson outlined the dilemma for the President,
tightening the regulations would provoke intense opposition from the
governors and social pressure groups. States that were already big winners would lose funds and others would be prevented from coming in.
Not tightening the regulations would require paying a very high price—
perhaps $6 billion or more in fiscal year 1974. One choice would be to
proceed with the administrative reforms already begun by the CSA, a

decision that would avoid a major political controversy but would achieve no significant savings. Another choice would be to require the expansion of state effort; federal funds would be available only to match new state funds. More restrictive still, an expansion-of-effort require-ment could be combined with a stricter definition of the scope of per-missible activity. Finally, the memorandum stated the possibility of phased implementation—proceeding before July 1 with the expansion-of-effort requirement, but postponing until after the election a stricter definition of services. This combination would seek "a balance between budget savings and political reaction."[8]

The President did choose a phased response, but not the one out-lined. He picked the first choice, in effect to do nothing for the short run, while letting it be known that he would crack down after the election. To the President's staff, it appeared in June that Congress might act, and that was certainly preferable both legally and politically. The President's office saw no point in incurring the political costs of a crackdown unnecessarily. To the HEW comptroller's office, by now intensely committed to achieving control, the President's choice came as a deep disappointment.

In Congress, alarm was rising. Politics in the distribution of funds was producing its own corrective. As more Republican governors suc-cessfully pressured a Republican administration into granting more funds, more Democrats developed an interest in limiting the volume of funds or at least influencing the distribution through legislation. New York's success, which the *New York Times* reported on page one in early June, in particular caught the attention of Senator Russell Long of Louisiana, chairman of the Senate Finance Committee. The committee promptly incorporated a $1 billion ceiling on services grants in House bill 1, the welfare reform bill, along with an allocation formula bene-ficial to states where the average per capita income was low. But House bill 1 was highly controversial and moving very slowly. The Senate did not begin debate on it until the end of September.

An early-summer effort by the Senate Appropriations Committee to achieve control came closer to succeeding. This committee, which had been relatively receptive to presidential requests for control in preceding years, in late June included a $2.5 billion ceiling in the HEW appro-priations bill for fiscal year 1973. This ceiling was dropped in confer-ence, however, at the insistence of Congressman George Mahon of Texas, whose state was just then negotiating for benefits. The failure of Congress to include the ceiling was cited by the President in August as one reason for his veto of the HEW appropriations bill. He declared then that "Congress must harness this multi-billion-dollar runaway program."[9]

The loophole was closed when the exploitation of it became absurd. The states killed the goose by asking too much.

In mid-July a rump meeting of the governors produced a new estimate of state requests for fiscal year 1973—$4.7 billion, which was more than twice HEW's latest estimate, itself based on state figures and only two months old. Nine states were projecting increases of more than 1,000 percent over their grants of 1971. Mississippi projected an increase of 42,118 percent (sic), and a sum that was more than half of the state's budget. It was all too much, even for a capital grown tolerant of federal deficits and state grantsmanship. This government blunder, hitherto obscure, suddenly became news. Within a two-week period in August, exposés appeared in the *Washington Post, New York Times, Wall Street Journal, National Observer,* and *U.S. News and World Report.* The *Post* article, "How the Feds Bought Mississippi," appeared first and set the pace and tone.[10] The Joint Economic Committee of Congress scheduled a public inquiry for mid-September.[11]

The administration's revenue-sharing bill, which was making its way through Congress in the summer of 1972, proved to be the vehicle for control. The prospect of revenue sharing increased congressional concern over services grants. Members of the Senate Finance Committee, who led the effort at control, reasoned that the states did not need both and that, if they received both, they could multiply their demands for services funds by drawing on shared revenues for their 25 percent matching share. The potential costs to the federal government were enormous. Revenue sharing also gave Congress something with which to bargain for the governors' agreement to closing the open end. The control of services grants could be made a condition of the passage of revenue sharing.[12]

The bill that passed in October (the State and Local Fiscal Assistance Act of 1972) placed a $2.5 billion annual ceiling on services grants and limited each state's share to its percentage of the national population. Ten years after the law had created it and within months after major exploitation by the states, the open end had been closed.[13]

CHAPTER NINE

Where the Controllers Were

PRECEDING SECTIONS have described how "the worst loophole" developed and how the states came to exploit it. With this history told, it is possible to return to the question stated at the start. Where were the executive agencies of control while all this was occurring? It has been possible to recount the story with only occasional reference to them. What did they do? Why did they fail? In particular, how did the President's own budget staff, the prestigious and reputedly powerful Office of Management and Budget (OMB), perform in this case?

At the time of the spending explosion, the OMB was overwhelmed by politics. Though appointive officials at the top of the OMB had stood firm against partisan pressures, Illinois was able to circumvent them with appeals to appointive officials in the Department of Health, Education, and Welfare (HEW), to the President, and to the President's White House staff. What needs to be explained in the performance of the OMB (and its predecessor agency, the Bureau of the Budget) is not its failure to prevent the exploitation of federal policies by a particular state, for this was not a failure of organizational function at all. It was quite simply political defeat—and defeat for the President's budget staff at such a point was thoroughly predictable, given the enormous opportunities inherent in the social services law and regulations, the power and vitality of big state governments as claimants on federal funds, the frequent indifference of U.S. senators and other members of Congress to presidential wish or party discipline when interests of their own constituents are at stake, and the pressures for payoffs and rewards that come to bear on a president when high offices, including his own, are soon to be at stake. What needs to be explained is the failure of the Budget Bureau and the OMB to prevent the development of federal policies that were so vulnerable to exploitation.

Even after allowing for the ordinary limits of human foresight, it is not unreasonable to expect that the President's staff might have discouraged the development of the loophole. In 1972, after the loophole had been discovered and exploited by the states, its existence was perfectly obvious to experienced observers and practitioners of government in Washington.* If it was so obvious in retrospect, why should it not have been obvious to the President's presumably expert staff at the time when laws and regulations were drafted and reviewed within the executive branch? Veteran public assistance administrators were nervous from the start about combining purchase with the open end; if they were concerned about exploitation by the states and private organizations, one might suppose that the Bureau of the Budget would have been even more concerned. Yet the perverse truth of the matter is that *purchase was the Budget Bureau's idea*, and the Budget Bureau pressed public assistance administrators to take a broad view of purchase at a time when the Bureau of Family Services (BFS) was reluctant to do so.

In theory, the Budget Bureau's first chance to arrest the development of the loophole should have come when legislation was prepared within the executive branch. An OMB circular requires executive agencies to submit proposed legislation or testimony on legislation for clearance.[1] These procedures are decades old. They do not prevent the executive departments from ever doing business with Congress behind the OMB's back, and they do not ensure that everything the departments submit to OMB is scrutinized with care, since the volume is large and time is limited. But they do mean that as a general rule the OMB gets a look in advance at what the departments will propose to Congress and can offer reactions that the departments may be expected to take into account. In fact, the Budget Bureau had ample opportunity to react to the Public Welfare Amendments of 1962, which laid the

---

* Indeed, professional colleagues have occasionally suggested to me that the focus of my inquiry is wrong, and that instead of asking how the loophole developed it would be more interesting to ask why the states were so slow to exploit it. That is a valid question. I believe that the states took a long time to exploit it because the initiative for exploitation rested for some years with welfare agencies, which understood the implicit limitations of the federal intent. They were inhibited by what they knew to be the purposes of their federal patron agency, the BFS. For exploitation to occur required that the BFS be deprived of jurisdiction at the federal level and that governors' budget offices or other grantsmen invade the traditional jurisdiction of welfare agencies at the state level.

basis for the loophole in services grants. Wilbur Cohen, who was directing preparation of the legislation for HEW, discussed his ideas with Budget Bureau officials even before he revealed them in the department.

Cohen had the basic elements of the legislation in mind by late September 1961. On the eve of a trip to Europe, he had sketched them out in brief hand-written notes for Sidney Saperstein, the department's legislative draftsman, who began to work up a draft in Cohen's absence. On Cohen's instructions, Saperstein did not discuss the proposals with anyone outside the general counsel's office. These early documents contain the idea that state welfare agencies should be induced to increase the giving of services. Cohen had in mind a new requirement that the states should develop a plan for services for each child on Aid to Dependent Children (ADC),* and should be offered a higher matching rate for giving services than for other administrative activities. There is no reference in this crude first draft either to extending services to former and potential recipients of aid or to authorizing the purchase of services from other state agencies, both of which became critical elements of the legal loophole.[2] These elements do not appear until a second draft of the legislation, which was prepared on October 26, two days after Cohen's meeting with the Budget Bureau.

The meeting covered general approaches to welfare legislation. There was no detailed discussion of a legislative text, since as yet there was no text, only a rough outline. The purpose was to agree on what should be in the text. Attending for the Budget Bureau were four members of the Labor and Welfare Division; for HEW, besides Cohen there were three members of the general counsel's office. Cohen opened by saying that he and the secretary wanted to expand rehabilitative services in the public assistance program. The Budget Bureau was interested in giving federal aid for general assistance, which it preferred to a further buildup of ADC. The bureau thought that this would be simpler and more flexible for the states and that a program of federal aid for general assistance might relieve pressure for more federal involvement in unemployment compensation. Cohen explained why the department preferred to expand ADC with aid for unemployed parents of ADC children. The bureau responded positively to Cohen's suggestion for a new emphasis on services. "There was general agreement," a record of this

* ADC became AFDC (Aid to Families with Dependent Children) in 1962.

meeting says, "that we should make a big push on rehabilitation services—broadening the character of the services, adding more attractive
matching, and perhaps imposing mandatory requirements on the
States." There was some discussion of jurisdictional issues. Cohen suggested that HEW give the Children's Bureau to the Department of
Labor in exchange for unemployment compensation. The Budget Bureau proposed transferring the peacetime veterans' rehabilitation service
program to the Office of Vocational Rehabilitation in HEW. And,
toward the end, the bureau "recommended that State public assistance
agencies be authorized to contract with State vocational rehabilitation
and other State agencies for rehabilitation services to public assistance
applicants or recipients." The record states that "Mr. Cohen seemed
sympathetic to this."[3]

The next day, Cohen gave Saperstein new instructions. The draft
was to provide for the purchase of services from state vocational rehabilitation and health agencies and for giving services to former and
potential as well as current recipients of assistance. Nothing in the
record of the meeting with the Budget Bureau suggests that eligibility
for former and potential recipients was discussed. It seems likely that
Cohen added it to the draft after being assured of the Budget Bureau's
general endorsement of the services approach. Thereafter, he began to
solicit comments from program units in HEW.

Between November 1, when clearance within the department began,
and February 1, when Secretary Ribicoff transmitted a bill to Congress,
the legislation went through repeated drafts and was reviewed several
times by the technical staff in the Budget Bureau. In contrast to HEW's
files, which contain evidence of Saperstein's concern about possible
pressures on the secretary to grant services funds and about the dangers
inherent in a loose definition of services, there is no sign that Budget
Bureau officials detected any risk in linking services grants to the open-
ended public assistance titles. The Budget Bureau's staff papers, unlike
HEW's, make no reference to the open-ended character of the public
assistance authorization. The bureau's principal staff review of the
legislation consisted of a summary of the HEW proposals along with a
proposal of two lower-cost alternatives to HEW measures for liberaliz-
ing eligibility and cash support of public assistance recipients. But on
such points as how much money should be spent and for what groups
of recipients, Cohen appears to have been getting his presidential-level

advice from outside the Budget Bureau. He was consulting with President Kennedy's counsel, Theodore Sorensen, who was prepared to approve measures that the Budget Bureau was inclined to resist. The legislation that President Kennedy sent to Congress in February 1962, after the bureau had formally cleared it as "in accord with the program of the President," and that the President signed in late July, bore few marks of the bureau's influence, unless one counts as such the provision for the purchase of services.[4]

After the law was enacted, the Budget Bureau persisted in encouraging public assistance agencies to purchase services. Purchase was not a fleeting notion, advanced casually in the meeting with Cohen only to be forgotten. In the fall of 1965, after attending a Budget Bureau hearing, an official of the Welfare Administration reported as follows to HEW's Office of General Counsel:

Yesterday at a budget hearing on public assistance grants, Budget Bureau staff indicated that they thought we could use the authority for 75% Federal matching for services more broadly than was being done under present policies in order to make greater efforts to reduce dependency. In particular, they believe that we can and should use these funds for such items as the purchase of educational, basic literacy, and vocational education services for welfare recipients and potential recipients, as well as the purchase of day-care services. In their opinion, this favorable matching rate should not apply just to staff of public welfare agencies but also to services provided by other agencies and financed by funds of welfare agencies.[5]

Accordingly, the Welfare Administration sought from HEW's lawyers an interpretation of its authority to use 75 percent matching for such purchases. The reply, prepared by Joel Cohen, stressed that purchase was difficult to use in many instances because the logical providers were private organizations, and the law authorized purchase from such organizations only indirectly, via state agencies other than those for public assistance.[6] Pressure from the Budget Bureau may help to account for the inclusion of authority for purchase from private sources in the Social Security Act Amendments of 1967. This became an important element of the loophole.

Otherwise, it is unlikely that the Budget Bureau had any influence on the statutory changes made in services grants in 1967 or that it gave any consideration to them. The services amendments were trivia, relatively speaking, which can barely be detected in the behemoth that became law in 1967. Also, Congress took considerably more initiative in 1967 than in 1962, which meant that much was decided in executive sessions on Capitol Hill to which the Budget Bureau was not invited. In such cases, Congress ordinarily seeks "technical consultation" from departmental representatives, and the routines of legislative clearance do not afford the Budget Bureau much access to important decisions.[7]

Given this legislative history and the lack of any perception in the Budget Bureau that services grants could pose a problem of control, it is not surprising that the bureau evinced no particular interest in regulations—the second point at which it might have arrested development of the loophole. Regulations, unlike legislation, are not subject to formal clearance by the OMB, which has issued no circular on the subject, yet the departments understand that the OMB should be informed of regulations that have major implications for expenditure. There is no evidence to indicate whether the Social and Rehabilitation Service (SRS) submitted the 1969 services regulations to the Budget Bureau, but even if it did so, it is altogether unlikely that the bureau would have raised objections. Manifestly, it would have approved the new emphasis on purchase and abandonment of the narrow conception of services as casework. The Budget Bureau's demand in 1965 was for a broader conception, better designed to reduce dependency. It would not have occurred to the Budget Bureau staff that the reorganization of 1967, which installed Mary Switzer as head of the SRS and reduced the influence of the rigid, rule-bound, traditional social workers who staffed the BFS, should have been the occasion for heightened scrutiny of public assistance administration. Mary Switzer's formidable reputation as a woman who produced results extended into the bureau as well as Congress. Within the bureau the reorganization inspired hope and confidence.

The Budget Bureau's failure to exert control at the stages of legislation and regulation left budgeting and the review of expenditures as the last point at which to conduct a defense, which by definition would be very hard to do with an uncontrollable item. Budget officials call an item uncontrollable when they have no discretion over its size but must meet obligations fixed in law. Nevertheless, the Budget Bureau might have influenced services spending by hard questioning of HEW officials in budget reviews. Indirectly, this might have affected administrative interpretations of the law.

A retired official of the BFS recalls that the Budget Bureau's examiner for public assistance in the late 1960s did regularly inquire into the results of the 1962 amendments, trying to ascertain what was being achieved by the higher matching rate for services. The examiner, Greg Barlous, was a veteran of many years in the Budget Bureau, where he had developed an extensive acquaintance with HEW programs and the people who ran them. He knew the vocational rehabilitation program especially well. In trying to judge the services amendments, Barlous went into the field unannounced, as was his wont, and observed intake services in a county welfare department in Maryland. The BFS official thought that Barlous was favorably impressed. If there was any disappointment in the Budget Bureau, it was that the BFS wasn't doing enough.

The OMB does not preserve the questions it asks of executive departments in budget reviews, but the character of its questioning may be inferred from what HEW officials, on the basis of experience, have learned to anticipate. The following is a list of questions that the executive officer of the Community Services Administration (CSA) prepared in October 1970 in the expectation that the OMB would ask them in budget hearings scheduled for the following week:

1. What do you know about services now that you did not know last year?

2. Do you have adequate reporting on services? What services reporting do you have?

3. What research and demonstration projects are underway or planned in the area of social services?

4. You recently put out a goals statement. Please explain what it is and what impact it has on your programs.

5. We understand that States are earmarking large sums for child care. What impact does this have on your social services budget? Can you mount a child care program large enough to meet the need?

6. If new social services legislation is enacted, how much staff would be needed in the central office and in the regional offices?

7. What is the status of separation [of services administration from administration of cash payments to welfare recipients]?

8. What is the extent of child welfare services being paid for under IV-A?*

* IV-A is the AFDC title of the Social Security Act, which the states were using more and more to pay for child welfare because the open-endedness and a higher matching ratio made it a more advantageous source than Title IV-B, the child welfare section of the Social Security Act.

9. Do you have any concrete examples of results of specific services? Of different service delivery systems?[8]

These anticipated questions, while faintly skeptical, were far from severe, and the one question that the CSA anticipated about the size of the services budget was linked with a question about whether the CSA would be able to do enough to meet the need for child care. It is not clear from these mock questions whether CSA officials believed that the OMB thought the CSA was spending too much or too little. (In the prepared answers, the CSA argued that success in child care depended on continuing the open-ended federal authorization.)

The Budget Bureau's failure to foresee difficulty in controlling services grants meant that it would not get alarmed until expenditure figures caused it to. Services grants rose rapidly in percentage terms between 1969 and 1971, but the actual totals in 1970 were still not very large by federal standards—on the order of $500 million—nor were the absolute annual increases large by comparison with those of other uncontrollable items in HEW's budget such as Medicaid and AFDC. Social services grants would have to attain a different order of magnitude before the OMB would feel that control was urgent.

In sum, in the decade from 1961 to 1970, as the loophole was developing, the Budget Bureau's routine processes of review failed to arrest it or to anticipate it at a time when it could have been prevented. For the Budget Bureau to allow this major uncontrollable item to develop surely was a failure of organizational function.

One reason for this failure was an inability to predict accurately the practical consequences of what the Budget Bureau itself proposed. Lacking experience in program administration, the bureau's staff did not foresee the potential for the exploitation of purchase when combined with the open end and the authorization pertaining to former and potential recipients. It would be easier to dismiss this as ordinary want of foresight but for the fact that experienced administrators in HEW, both in the BFS and the Office of General Counsel, did sense the danger. Because it is far removed from the field, the President's staff inevitably has a limited comprehension of the real consequences of administrative acts. In promoting purchase, the bureau was not indifferent to expenditure control; it was ignorant of the implications of what it was promoting.

Yet the bureau's commitment to expenditure control was ambiguous, and this too must enter into an explanation of its failure. The bureau's functions and priorities had changed over the years. Founded in 1921, the Budget Bureau developed initially as an institutional nay-sayer, a stern and consistent critic of federal spending. As such, it could not have survived as the staff of post–New Deal presidents. The adaptation that occurred has been well described by a long-time bureau member, Phillip S. Hughes:

It's very hard for me to say that, you know, on 'x' date we had a philosophical change. I'm sure the historians will describe it that way at some point, but I'm too much in the trees to see the forest in that kind of perspective. Over the years, and I think it started in the middle or the later part of the Eisenhower Administration, the role of the Bureau has changed somewhat; as government grew, as it did in the Eisenhower Administration and subsequently, the Bureau has acquired a programming role that it did not have, at least to the same extent, before. The problem of choice among the programs has become increasingly important. And perhaps, to some extent, the negative role of the Bureau has become less important, at least in relative terms. And the agencies themselves are more responsible than they used to be for efficient and economic operation. . . .

The Bureau has looked at itself and looked at government programs in a somewhat different light. In the old days, speaking in very oversimplified terms, our initial answer was supposed to be no, and everybody would have been surprised if we said yes the first time around. As time has passed, we're supposed to do something a little different than that. We can say no, perhaps in a fairly high percentage of cases, but in some of the more crucial ones we're supposed to give pretty serious consideration to alternative and better ways of accomplishing an objective which the President or an agency had or a member of the majority party in the Congress thinks is a desirable objective. And so we have increasingly tried to give consideration to how to do something rather than lining up a long list of reasons why it shouldn't be done.[9]

That the bureau increasingly thought in terms of achieving the President's programmatic objectives did not mean that it ceased to value efficiency of expenditure. In conceiving programs and putting choices before the President, it characteristically sought the most efficient designs or defined choices of lower cost than those the departments proposed. This may help to explain its interest in the purchase of services. It wanted to secure a public objective—the reduction of welfare dependency. It took more or less at face value the arguments of HEW that rehabilitative services would reduce dependency, since no one had a better idea and the Budget Bureau judged vocational rehabilitation programs to be highly successful. It also favored purchase as a technique because it did not want to encourage the multiplication or overlap of federal and state bureaucracies.

In pursuit of programmatic objectives, the bureau began to give new kinds of cues to the executive departments. It urged them to do more of what the President had said was important and the bureau believed to be promising; it would ask in budget reviews if they had enough money for such programs. If the function of expenditure control was not sacrificed in the course of this change, it was compromised. Bureau staff increasingly turned their attention to other things ("program development") and defined their purposes in other terms ("preserving choice"). In regard to services grants, the bureau apparently attached greater importance to promoting measures to reduce welfare dependency than to scrutinizing such measures for defects in fiscal control.

And yet the Budget Bureau staff was not wholly without foresight in the matter of social services spending, and it was very much concerned during the late 1960s with the general problem of uncontrollability, of which social services grants were an example. It was, in fact, the bureau's generalized concern with "controlling the uncontrollables" in the HEW budget that spurred the first attempts by the executive branch to close the open-ended authorization for social services grants. These attempts antedated the spending explosion of 1971–72 by well over a year.

Briefing papers prepared by career staff of the Budget Bureau for the incoming administration in 1969 stressed the built-in growth potential of HEW programs; without mentioning services specifically, these papers cited public assistance as the most uncontrollable area. Newly arrived Republicans at the top of the bureau, especially Richard Nathan, proved to be quite responsive to these cues. Very early in the administration, Nathan began trying to convince Secretary Finch of the need to do something about HEW's uncontrollables lest they deprive the administration of room for initiative. In response to this pressure from the President's office, HEW Comptroller James F. Kelly improvised a way to control services spending. Kelly's idea was to limit grants to each state in any one year to 110 percent of what they had been in the preceding year through the HEW appropriations act. Under Secretary Veneman approved this idea over objections from the SRS and from Tom Joe, who by his own account "fought it tooth and nail." The proposal became part of the President's budget in fiscal year 1971 and, though defeated then, was reintroduced the following year.

Among HEW's various uncontrollables, the department's comptroller picked out the budget item for social services because he thought it the most promising candidate for control. In that particular case, he could think of something to do, and he could see no good arguments for not doing it. Even those who argued against closing the open end, like Joe, did not argue against it in principle. They only argued that the timing was wrong or that the method was unrealistic and inequitable because it would limit have-not states.

There were good reasons for the open-endedness of grants for cash assistance to the poor, since no one could know how many recipients there would be, but the same logic did not apply to services, which consisted largely of administrative costs. Marshalling this and other arguments, Secretary Richardson (Finch's successor) and Bruce Cardwell (Kelly's successor) urged Congress in the summer of 1970 to adopt the 110 percent limit. Said Richardson: "The time . . . to put a cap on this uncontrolled flow of appropriations is now. . . . the situation resulting from the open-ended appropriation has gotten entirely out of hand . . . we in the Capital have a national responsibility. I think this one is really one [where] we can draw a line on expenditures."[10] Cardwell positively pleaded with the Senate Appropriations Committee to act:

I have, as an individual, worked with this committee in one capacity or another for 15 years. . . .

During that time, I don't think I have made any special pleas as an individual, but this is one case, not out of partisan reasons, but this is one case where I would implore the committee to stop, look, and listen.

If you look at the HEW budget, and I am looking a year ahead, such a large share of it is what is really known as uncontrollable costs . . . there isn't going to be any elbow room under this administration or any administration to do some of the things that we need to do. Really, this is an effort, for the first time, to put a lid on one of these costs. . . .

Unless we learn how to do this with this one example, we are in serious trouble. . . . It is probably the most important item, as a precedent, in the total HEW budget.[11]

It was too late. California had already taken advantage of the loophole, and pressures were building from other states. Governors barraged Congress with objections to the limit. As Senator Norris Cotton, a supporter of the limit, later said: "There was not a prayer of getting the 110-percent limitation. . . . the trouble is that every Member of the Congress—every Senator—would find out that his State would lose something, and we didn't have a hope."[12] The House Appropriations Committee twice rejected the administration's request for the ceiling.[13] The Senate Appropriations Committee twice recommended a ceiling of 115 percent, but the full Senate voted against it, 57 to 20 in 1970 and 50 to 40 in 1971. (The vote in 1971 was on a ceiling of 120 percent, which had been substituted for the 115 percent limit on the floor.) Once made aware of the loophole, Congress was certainly in no hurry to close it. Indeed, in view of the failure of Congress to act in 1970 and 1971, it may be misleading thereafter to speak of a "loophole." The sharp growth of federal expenditure that occurred then was not of itself clearly contrary to congressional intent.

Statutory control was what the executive control agencies were hoping for, either through the appropriations act, the route the HEW comptroller had devised, or through new services legislation, which Nathan from his office in the OMB was urging HEW to prepare. Nathan thought of new services legislation, to be incorporated in the Family Assistance Plan, as another way in which the open end could be closed, and a legislative proposal was ready in the summer of 1970. That the Family Assistance Plan had passed the House in the spring of 1970 made this seem a promising strategy. But like the 110 percent limitation, new services legislation did not get anywhere in Congress.

When it seemed that attempts to close the open end through legislation were doomed, technical staff in the Human Resources Programs Division of the OMB began casting about for something else to do. Their effort may have been triggered by the appearance early in 1971 of the Booz, Allen and Hamilton report on the purchase of services, which contained some revealing, because very detailed, passages on how private agencies were refinancing their activities with federal funds.[14] When Diana Zentay, OMB examiner of the public assistance programs, read that report, a light dawned. So that was how it was done! She and her immediate superior, William Robinson, assistant division chief in charge of income maintenance and veterans' affairs, set up some meetings with Stephen Simonds and his staff in the CSA to talk about how the administration of services funds might be improved.

Robinson and Zentay approached their jobs in a very different way from the veteran Barlous, who died early in 1970. Their milieu was Washington, and their mode was analytical. They held advanced degrees from leading graduate schools, had won prestigious fellowships, and had prior government experience in fiscal analysis or program planning. In 1970–71, they were frantically busy with the U.S. government's ultimate challenge to analytic skills—welfare reform—in which Nathan, their superior, was deeply involved. New to their jobs, both had had to learn the subject matter. Zentay had started work without knowing what public assistance was; Robinson had to master, not just public assistance, but railroad retirement benefits, veterans' pensions, food stamps, and social security. For both, monitoring social services grants was low on a long list of things to do; and unlike the planning of the Family Assistance Plan, services grants did not intrude insistently into their daily routine, demanding quick answers to complex questions. Besides, overseeing the details of departmental operations was not the OMB's proper business in Robinson's view. He thought the OMB was constantly in danger of being ensnared by the particular, whereas its special competence lay with the general and the conceptual.

Despite their preoccupation with other matters, Robinson and Zentay were sufficiently alert to services spending to have scheduled the meetings with Simonds and his staff in the spring of 1971. Their reaction to these encounters with the CSA was much like that of Illinois officials: pure frustration. One of them later remarked that it was like walking in fudge. They could not make any headway, and, while Simonds was personally the most cooperative of men, they constantly had the sense that at least some of the staff in the CSA were out to undo them.

Undo them the department surely did, with the June 17 memorandum. If their meetings with the CSA had any effect at all, it was probably the reverse of what they intended. The pressure from the OMB may have increased Simonds's disposition to issue something without, however, having any discernible effect on the substance of what was issued. It is hard to charge the OMB with a failure of organizational performance at this point. Its staff could not reasonably be expected to have done more, given the responsibility of the departments for the administration of expenditures, or to have succeeded better, given the force of the Illinois governor as a counterpressure on offices higher than that of the CSA commissioner.

To summarize, in 1970–71 the OMB perceived that a loophole

existed in regard to services grants and elicited legislative proposals from HEW for closing it, but these proposals failed for want of support in Congress. The OMB did not succeed in eliciting effective administrative controls from HEW. Quite the contrary; the action that was forthcoming from program units in the department sharply accelerated state claims. The OMB lacked reliable access to policymaking within the department. That its staff was preoccupied with matters other than expenditure control was true but probably incidental to the outcome.

The limits on the OMB's ability to influence the departments along with the declining emphasis that the OMB places cn fiscal control mean that if the executive branch is to secure such control over any program, it must be done very largely within the departments. As Hughes observed, "The agencies themselves are more responsible than they used to be for efficient and economic operation." The question is whether their capacities match their responsibility in this respect.

HEW's capacity for planning the use of its funds presumably was improving in the late 1960s as the Office of the Assistant Secretary for Planning and Evaluation developed. Added to the department in 1966 following President Johnson's government-wide order to establish planning, programming, and budgeting systems (PPBS), this office "coordinates Department activities in economic and social analysis, program analysis and planning, and evaluation activities, and ensures that the results of these activities are appropriately reflected in Department policy and program planning."[15] Its actual functions have varied considerably with changes of administration and individual officeholders; just how far and how successfully economic and social analysis can be injected into the department's policymaking remains an open question, and different secretaries and assistant secretaries for planning and evaluation have gone about it in different ways. In keeping with the mission of PPBS, the office initially sought to establish an orderly long-range planning process that would discipline annual budgetary and legislative decisions throughout the department. This proved very difficult to do, and the forms and procedures of PPBS were quietly abandoned following the change of administrations.[16]

In the first years of the Nixon administration, the office as a whole atrophied while, paradoxically, the assistant secretary became much more influential than before. The incumbent, a Californian, was on close, friendly terms with both Secretary Finch and Under Secretary

Veneman, as well as with some of the White House staff, and personally played a large part in making the administration's policies for health, education, and welfare. In doing so, however, he did not particularly nurture the specialized capacities of the office he headed. Richardson, as secretary, was determined to develop the analytical competence of the office and named as assistant secretary an economist with considerable experience in policy analysis. The office then set out to tackle "basic conceptual problems that cut across the department," one of its members later recalled. Rather than try to cover the whole department or review the whole budget, it selected a few issues of broad scope that seemed likely to benefit from abstract analysis. One man was assigned to social services, but not to examine the utility of current expenditures or to demand justifications from the SRS. In keeping with the mission of the office and Richardson's own interests, this man was supposed to design a new "social services delivery system"—one that would rationalize the chaotic universe of overlapping professional specialties that so dismayed the secretary.

Beginning in the late 1960s, some members of the office were aware of the explosive potential of the open-ended legislation, for routine reviews of the budget had revealed the sharp rise in expenditures and California's disproportionate receipt of funds. The Office for Planning and Evaluation did contribute to planning the legislation that would have closed the open end, but in general it was only a tangential and occasional participant in decisions on services grants. In none of its various phases did it combine purpose, influence, and staff skills in a way that would have enabled it to initiate controls over services spending.

Within HEW, the principal agent of expenditure control is the Office of the Comptroller, which is part of the Office of the Secretary. The comptroller is one of eight assistant secretaries; in 1974, his office consisted of units for budgeting, finance, and auditing. The finance and auditing units are concerned mainly with review of expenditure ex post facto, and auditing is based mainly in the field. Prior review, the kind that might prevent or contain the development of an uncontrollable item, is located in the budget office.

Budget officials review legislative proposals but ordinarily only for the limited purpose of clearing whatever cost estimates may accompany them. In 1961 the comptroller saw and approved a one-page table of

Bureau of Public Assistance (BPA) gross estimates of the cost of the proposed Public Welfare Amendments of 1962.* The comptroller does not usually make independent estimates of cost or review in detail the regulations issued by HEW's program units. In theory, the comptroller's office is responsible for reviewing regulations. In practice, the large volume of regulations and the limited size of the comptroller's staff, as well as that staff's limited ability to grasp the operational implications of regulations, has made the reviews meaningless.

It is possible that someone in the comptroller's office saw the 1969 regulations for services before they were issued but unlikely that he would have known their significance. The Budget Division did not then have a staff member who specialized in welfare programs. Welfare was a part-time responsibility of the man who was in charge of reviewing the budget of the Social Security Administration. Even more than the Budget Bureau or the OMB, which at least had a well-developed procedure for legislative review, the HEW comptroller's office focused its prior reviews of expenditure on the budget process, a late stage, and thus was in a poor position to bring any influence to bear on an uncontrollable. When confronted with services grants, the best thing that Kelly and Cardwell could think of to do was to try to convert the uncontrollable item into a controlled item with the 110 percent ceiling, which failed in Congress.

On the other hand, within the department the comptroller's staff was not passive as social services spending grew. It counted heavily on the 110 percent proposal but did not use that as an excuse for doing nothing else. As it happened, in 1969 the comptroller's office had added a full-time specialist in welfare programs—a young man named Earl Canfield who moved over from a job elsewhere in HEW to become chief of the Social and Rehabilitation Services branch in the Division of Budget. Besides Canfield, the branch consisted of an analyst and a management intern. This marked an evolution in the capacity of the budget staff, and Canfield's presence was very important when finally the executive branch seriously contemplated bringing services spending

---

* The table did not identify services costs separately. Elsewhere, the BPA estimated that the services provisions of the Public Welfare Amendments of 1962 would cost $88.6 million in 1967. It is hard to judge the accuracy of this estimate because in the actual budget for fiscal year 1967 services grants were lumped with grants for administration and training.

under control. Had he not been there, and had he not been a singularly conscientious and thoughtful man—confident of his own purposes yet capable of cooperation with others—HEW's capacity to exert control would have been even less than it was during the spending explosion.

Canfield at first approached the subject of services, as any sensible budget officer might, by trying to find out what the money was going for. In the summer of 1970 he had the help of an intern, a college student, whom he assigned to that task. They could learn nothing. The CSA's persistent inability to account for the spending—whether to the HEW comptroller, the OMB, or the White House task force that considered services legislation—increased the anxiety of the control agencies. The problem was not just that the volume of spending was growing fast and unpredictably and had no limit in law. No one knew what was being done with the money. Pressure from the control agencies finally prompted the CSA to hire the private accounting firm, Touche Ross and Company, to do a study.[17] Without this study, there would be practically no evidence on the subject.

It was not until the fall of 1971 that Canfield was able to come to grips with services spending and to start bringing the influence of the comptroller's office to bear on the department's administrative actions —and then he could do so only because of an opportunity that presented itself in the Illinois case. Though he had had no part in any of the earlier deliberations over Illinois and knew nothing of them or of the June 17 memorandum, he was invited to attend the late-September meeting at which the Illinois plan proposals were presented. To the best of his recollection, he was there at the invitation of Joe, whom he had come to regard as a friend and who, he later surmised, was beginning to feel a bit exposed in his role as sponsor of services spending. As a newcomer to the case, Canfield was in no position to say much on that occasion, but the meeting turned out to be a pivotal event, the beginning of an effort by HEW to make new rules to govern services spending.

Following the acrimonious meeting with Illinois officials, Joe sent a short, angry account of it to Under Secretary Veneman. Having listened to the Illinois officials' plans for services funds, Joe was feeling ill-used, and Canfield was aroused and alarmed. It seemed clear to Canfield that Illinois was going to refinance state activities with federal funds on a large scale, that other states would inevitably follow, and that HEW simply had to put a stop to it. (He did not know how committed the department already was in the Illinois case, and of course he could not foresee the concession that the President's office would make two months later under the threat of the Percy amendment.)

Overnight, Joe and Canfield drafted a memorandum for Veneman to send to John Twiname, administrator of the SRS. Sent on September 28, the very day that Simpson signed the Illinois plan amendments, this document conveyed a genuine sense of urgency. It instructed Twiname to "take fast and effective actions to correct existing situations and prevent their amplification in the future." He was to reply by October 15 and to issue new regulations by January 1, to take effect on July 1. Among other things the new regulations should be designed to "generate basic program information concerning types of services rendered, cost of particular services compared to numbers and types of recipients, etc.," and to "enable SRS and HEW to exercise reasonable stewardship of Federal funds and identify and pursue compliance issues." States should be required "to submit a program budget for social services, backed by a separate accounting system that will support program and financial audits." Joe had long expressed a concern over the need for better planning, budgeting, and accounting by state governments in regard to services; for him, this memorandum was not a reversal, but it was a distinct change in emphasis in response to the rapidly developing demands of the states.

The following spring a flock of task forces in the CSA produced new regulations in response to Veneman's memorandum. On reviewing them, Canfield concluded that they would only make matters worse. Having educated himself on the subject of social services, he was able to counter the CSA proposals with concrete suggestions. The result was a stalemate in HEW between the SRS and the comptroller's office and then a decision by the President to postpone executive control of services spending until after the election and to encourage action by Congress in the interim. Without backing from the White House, the comptroller's office did not secure the new and more effective regulations it sought, but by opposing the CSA's proposed regulations, at least it raised issues for consideration by the under secretary and secretary and enabled them to take account of fiscal problems when contemplating the CSA proposals.*

* CSA officials, one later said, understood the September 28 memorandum to be a call for improved accountability, for that was how Joe and Bax interpreted it to

From its base within the department and with its more specialized competence, the HEW comptroller's office was much more effectively involved in controlling services spending than was the President's staff; but like the OMB, it came very late to the case and was unable to detect and arrest the loophole at the stage of development. For both organizations, control ordinarily focuses on the budget process; annually, they ask of program units: why are you spending more? Ordinarily, they have only an indirect and limited influence on decisions that lead to spending. If expenditure control is to be weighed in such decisions, it must be done by the agencies with direct responsibility for program administration—the Social and Rehabilitation Service, in the case of social services grants.

The SRS consists of several program units with a layer of generalist staff on top. It was organized near the end of the Johnson administration with the following objectives (emphasis supplied):

(i) To develop a *unified approach* to the delivery of services to individuals and families.

(ii) To place primary emphasis on *rehabilitation* and the reduction or prevention of dependency.

(iii) To place increased *authority* for decision-making *in the regional offices*.

(iv) To *simplify*, as far as possible, the *relations between the Federal Government and the state agencies* participating in programs assigned to the SRS.

(v) To place increased emphasis on developing *new ways* of organizing and delivering services.[18]

In brief, the key terms were coordination, decentralization (within the federal administrative structure and in federal-state relations), and innovation, and these were combined with a programmatic emphasis on rehabilitation. Efficiency, economy, good management, or fiscal control were not among the objectives; these were key terms for other times and other places. The functions of the generalist staff at the top of the SRS reflected the objectives of the reorganization. Assistant administrators began to multiply, but none was charged with fiscal management. Six assistants in 1969–70 had the functions of administration, federal-state relations, field operations, program planning and evalua-

---

them. The CSA, according to this source, did not understand that new regulations were supposed "to plug up the big holes created by June 17," and plugging these holes was Canfield's objective.

tion, research and development and training, and public affairs. That the SRS initially attached a higher value to simplifying federal-state relations and to decentralizing federal administration than to controlling expenditures goes far toward explaining what happened to social services grants.

A Republican administration might have been expected to alter the emphasis, and it did—but not right away. It was not until the spring of 1971 that an Office of Financial Management was located in the SRS and an assistant administrator put at the head of it, charged specifically to improve the control of expenditures. Had it come somewhat earlier, this organizational change might have stayed the uncontrolled outburst of services spending. As it was, the change gave the SRS some capacity to respond quickly when the explosion occurred.*

The first assistant commissioner for financial management was Francis D. DeGeorge, whose previous experience had been entirely in private organizations. After getting out of the Marine Corps in the early 1950s, he had been manager of cost accounting in the explosives department of DuPont. Simultaneously, he worked on a master's degree in business administration at the University of Delaware. Thereafter he had held jobs in cost accounting and control in half a dozen companies large and small. He was ambitious ("hungry," someone in HEW said), without being in the least unpleasant, and he was straightforward, even unsophisticated, in his approach to his job. DeGeorge knew no jargon; he simply thought that the federal government should get something for its money. Without party connections, he got the job in HEW because he went looking for it, and his inexperience in government turned out to be something of an asset. He did not know what could not be done.

For something over a year starting late in 1971, Canfield and DeGeorge worked as a team to bring social services spending under control. After his arrival in March 1971, it took DeGeorge a while to come to grips with the problem, which was only then beginning to develop in a dramatic way. (DeGeorge's arrival in HEW roughly coincided with the delivery of Governor Ogilvie's budget message for fiscal year 1972 to the Illinois Assembly.) He had been briefed by Paul O'Neill of the OMB on the need to control the uncontrollables, and he learned in

---

* See appendix B for a chart of the organization of SRS in 1971.

the spring that services grants were a trouble spot, but it was not until an encounter with the Illinois case at summer's end that he determined that something must be done. For him, the precipitating incident was a report by Owen Ash, chief of the state fiscal standards branch in the Assistance Payments Administration, who had gone out to the SRS Chicago regional office as a consultant on the Illinois case. He was supposed to advise the regional staff on how to calculate federal financial participation under the pending state plan. The costs involved, the problems in accounting, and the dangers in calculating costs retroactively "just hit me very heavily," Ash later said. At the end of August he wrote an account of these to Commissioner Bax of the CSA; a copy went to DeGeorge. Here, possibly for the first time, the implications of the Illinois case were explained by an experienced civil servant in the hard terms of the dollars at stake and the hard problems of administration and cost accounting that the SRS was getting into. The Ash memo galvanized DeGeorge and had an effect elsewhere in the SRS. It helps to explain the firm stand that program units took against granting the single-state-agency waivers.

DeGeorge and Canfield began by proposing to add more than 400 fiscal management positions to the SRS staff. The SRS's total employment was then around 2,100. Accepted by the secretary's office and by the OMB, this proposal was put before Congress early in 1972 as part of an $800 million request by the SRS for supplemental appropriations. (More than half of this supplemental was for social services grants.) Ultimately, only 210 of the 427 new positions actually went for fiscal management, and DeGeorge had to fight hard in the SRS for those. Of the 210, 180 were placed in the regions. The SRS had established the new position of assistant regional commissioner for financial management and was proposing to place financial managers in the state capitals, backed by staff in the regional offices. Creating a fiscal presence in the regions was "unique in welfare management," the SRS told Congress. "We do not have this and never had it in the regional office before; fiscal people, financial management people, not social workers or program development people."[19] If the SRS had had such a presence in Chicago, something like the Ash memorandum might have been written sooner; if it had had such a presence in all the regions, estimates of the cost of state plans presumably would have been developed routinely. At headquarters. many of the positions went to a new Division of State

Grants Administration. Among the division's many functions, one was to

review proposed and existing legislation and federal regulations, providing comments on the financial implications of proposals and developing implementing instructions to exercise the financial controls necessary for effective administration of the law and regulations.[20]

Another step was to reduce the states' requests for social services grants by nearly $900 million in the second quarter of fiscal year 1973. This was an act of great significance, for it indicated some measure of intention by HEW to act as if services grants *were* controllable. Ordinarily in the public assistance program, states send quarterly estimates of their requests for federal matching funds to HEW, which sends these estimates without change to the Treasury Department, and the Treasury obligates funds in the amount of the estimate. Two quarters later, there is a settlement on the basis of what the states have "earned" by actual expenditure. Operationally, this was the essence of uncontrollability. But when the states in the late summer of 1972 submitted a quarterly estimate for services grants far exceeding that of previous quarters, DeGeorge proposed that it not be done that way any more. His office reviewed the claims and reduced them, with backing from Canfield and above him Cardwell, who in turn solicited approval from the OMB. This was done before Congress had enacted the $2.5 billion ceiling. HEW still would pay whatever the states earned, but reducing the estimates discouraged them from trying to earn all they said they would. At this point, estimates were rising so fast that HEW officials had every reason to believe that the alleged earnings were being achieved by accounting tricks, not by actual increases in services.

Finally, DeGeorge and Randolph W. Lee, director of the Division of State Grants Administration, with the help of Joel Cohen and the backing of Canfield, prepared a fresh statement of SRS policies regarding federal matching of state costs for services. After the presidential election in November, the Nixon White House was willing to take the heat that would come with control, and on December 20 the SRS issued a memorandum that reinterpreted federal regulations. Like the June 17 memorandum, this was an informal issuance, addressed to SRS regional commissioners, not the states, but in contrast to the June 17 memorandum it was signed by Twiname and there was no subsequent equivocation about it at headquarters. This one was not to be labeled "draft."

It too had a considerable impact on state behavior, this time in the direction of restraint, not expansion.

The December 20 memorandum was an accountant's document. It set forth restrictions on claims for residential care and on group services, and it asserted the responsibility of the single state agency for determining eligibility and developing service plans for individuals. (Individual service plans were required under the AFDC title of the Social Security Act, but this provision had been ignored as the conception of services as casework was abandoned.) The document came down very hard against granting retroactive claims for reimbursement. It said that accounting methods could not be constructed after the fact, nor could retroactive determinations of individual eligibility be allowed.[21] Using this memorandum as a basis, HEW began denying reimbursement for retroactive claims.

Between fiscal years 1972 and 1973, federal services spending dropped from $1.68 billion to $1.54 billion. The biggest winners in the game of grantsmanship suffered cuts because of Congress's formula that based the award of funds on population. New York got $388 million less than in 1972 and Illinois, $65 million less, but most states got more, including California, which was not adversely affected by the population formula. Even those states that advanced their grant totals, however, did not advance in most cases as far as the $2.5 billion ceiling and the population formula imposed by Congress would have permitted. Executive controls were apparently effective in slowing the increase, which indicates that they could have been effective sooner if they had been applied sooner. Table 2 (see pages 100–101) presents data on expenditures by state and shows the effects of the statutory ceiling imposed in 1972.

TABLE 2. *Federal Grants for Social Services, by State*

Thousands of dollars

State	Fiscal year 1971	Fiscal year 1972	Fiscal year 1973	Share allotted under State and Local Fiscal Assistance Act of 1972ᵃ
Alabama	7,142	11,697	16,651	42,140
Alaska	1,900	4,208	5,895	3,902
Arizona	2,829	2,748	3,238	23,351
Arkansas	2,145	3,273	6,276	23,747
California	190,334	198,627	227,321	245,733
Colorado	10,848	18,908	22,006	28,298
Connecticut	6,968	9,399	20,854	37,002
Delaware	2,844	12,456	6,593	6,873
District of Columbia	7,041	10,479	8,271	8,980
Florida	13,127	42,708	43,535	87,150
Georgia	12,083	32,415	48,095	56,667
(Guam)	(138)	(176)	(161)	(...)
Hawaii	698	847	2,365	9,713
Idaho	1,218	1,544	4,707	9,076
Illinois	43,546	188,381	123,444	135,077
Indiana	2,564	6,532	7,252	63,522
Iowa	6,826	9,536	12,657	34,613
Kansas	5,803	6,210	6,902	27,109
Kentucky	6,404	12,709	30,478	39,607
Louisiana	9,244	29,505	20,843	44,661
Maine	3,969	6,536	8,678	12,354
Maryland	15,004	20,946	26,661	48,695
Massachusetts	10,525	23,035	16,828	69,477
Michigan	16,407	28,039	48,220	109,036
Minnesota	19,175	26,587	30,264	46,774
Mississippi	947	1,833	11,540	27,169
Missouri	11,948	12,839	15,366	57,063
Montana	2,115	2,959	3,830	8,632
Nebraska	5,825	7,352	9,146	18,309
Nevada	1,004	1,616	1,753	6,327
New Hampshire	2,048	2,824	4,040	9,257
New Jersey	29,968	36,930	44,112	88,446
New Mexico	3,654	3,680	7,871	12,786
New York	67,296	588,929	200,616	200,497
North Carolina	13,004	19,470	24,373	62,598

TABLE 2 (*continued*)

State	Fiscal year 1971	Fiscal year 1972	Fiscal year 1973	Share allotted under State and Local Fiscal Assistance Act of 1972 [a]
North Dakota	2,464	3,325	3,951	7,588
Ohio	11,079	19,517	41,636	129,458
Oklahoma	7,519	14,060	24,805	31,623
Oregon	34,366	25,297	20,334	26,197
Pennsylvania	36,661	51,293	88,210	143,180
(Puerto Rico)	(4,384)	(3,261)	(1,847)	(...)
Rhode Island	4,682	6,623	9,391	11,622
South Carolina	3,089	6,031	9,752	31,995
South Dakota	2,049	2,377	2,469	8,152
Tennessee	10,229	13,835	23,483	48,395
Texas	12,962	53,500	94,672	139,855
Utah	3,069	4,084	5,542	13,519
Vermont	1,643	2,433	3,201	5,547
(Virgin Islands)	(305)	(368)	(440)	(...)
Virginia	10,184	16,262	21,523	57,195
Washington	33,695	34,308	56,731	41,336
West Virginia	7,948	7,373	8,156	21,382
Wisconsin	17,298	37,937	54,295	54,266
Wyoming	715	590	1,005	4,142
Total	740,958	1,688,432	1,542,312	2,500,000

Sources: *Social Services Regulations,* Hearings before the Senate Committee on Finance, 93 Cong. 1 sess. (1973), pt. 1, table 1, pp. 71–73; and U.S. Department of Health, Education, and Welfare, Social and Rehabilitation Service, Office of Financial Management, *State Expenditures for Public Assistance Programs Approved under Titles I, IV-A, X, XIV, XVI, and XIX of the Social Security Act,* for fiscal years 1971, 1972, and 1973.

a. The main purpose of the act was to authorize general revenue sharing. The figures represent entitlements under the $2.5 billion ceiling imposed by the act, as determined by a formula based on shares of the population. They are not actual expenditures.

CHAPTER TEN

The Reaction to Controls

THE STORY of social services spending does not end with Congress's closing of the open end in October 1972 and with the more or less simultaneous efforts of executive controllers in the Department of Health, Education, and Welfare (HEW). A new and different phase followed, marked by federal-state conflict and executive-legislative conflict as the states and Congress reacted sharply to the executive's attempts at control. Begun late in the first term of the Nixon administration, these attempts intensified in 1973, since in its second term the administration attached more importance to fiscal conservatism than it did in the first.

By mid-1974, eighteen states had filed seven suits against HEW because of the department's actions on social services. Covington and Burling on behalf of thirteen states was asking the U.S. District Court of the District of Columbia to enjoin the December 20 memorandum, charging that it was "arbitrary, capricious, an abuse of discretion, in excess of statutory authority" and had been promulgated "without complying with procedures required by law."[1] Six states were suing individually in an attempt to validate claims for retroactive reimbursement.[2] (One state, Idaho, was both a party to the joint suit and an individual litigant. Its administrator of environmental and community services was James A. Bax, who had left Washington for Boise.)

The executive-legislative conflict developed when the Social and Rehabilitation Service (SRS) tried to issue new regulations. In this it appeared initially to have congressional backing. Both the conference report on the revenue-sharing bill and the Senate Finance Committee's report on House bill 1, the Social Security Amendments of 1972, had instructed the secretary of HEW to issue regulations governing the purchase of services, and the Finance Committee instructed him as well to "clearly state that the State matching requirement cannot be met by funds donated by private sources."[3] Published early in 1973, HEW's proposed new regulations provoked a storm of protest from congressmen, governors, a host of public and private welfare organizations, and individuals. In two months the department received over 200,000 letters. A social services coalition of sixteen national welfare organizations was formed to concert opposition to the regulations, which would have eliminated group eligibility, ended the use of private funds in lieu of state matching funds, cut back on the services states were required to provide, narrowed the definition of former and potential recipients, and limited eligibility for services to assistance recipients or persons whose incomes put them near dependency. Private-agency opposition to the changes was particularly effective. Purchase from private organizations, which was nowhere near as important monetarily as purchase from public ones, turned out to be very important politically. Congressmen who had once demanded the closing of the loophole decided that it should be kept open a bit to permit community good works to continue. Representative Robert H. Michel of Illinois, a Republican, reflected on the situation in Peoria:

I found to my dismay that a number of my friends who are involved in all this volunteer work are going to be shut out from doing their thing for the community. I readily agreed that it appeared we actually were discouraging the private money going into child day-care services. I had forgot about how I raised "heck" about this open-ended thing on the floor. . . . Needless to say, I had to backtrack a bit.[4]

In the face of so much protest from so many respectable sources, HEW backed down and softened the proposed regulations at several points. But it did not back down enough to satisfy Congress, which in June 1973 postponed the new regulations until November 1, and in December postponed them until 1975.[5] In late December 1974, after prolonged negotiation with the administration, Congress enacted new social services legislation, and in early 1975 HEW began preparing regulations to implement this law, which retained the $2.5 billion ceiling on annual federal spending but gave the states wide latitude in determining the use of these funds.[6]

In addition to its futile attempt in 1974 to issue new regulations, the Nixon administration took more fundamental steps in response to the experience of services grants and, presumably, other experience as well.

Within HEW there was a wholesale change of top-level appointees, beginning with a new secretary, Caspar W. Weinberger, who had most recently been director of the Office of Management and Budget (OMB). Like their predecessors of 1969, many of the new Nixon appointees in HEW came from the West Coast. It was still a California crowd, but it was a very different California crowd. The men of 1973 were the fiscal controllers who had fought the liberalization of California welfare programs in the late 1960s and administered Governor Ronald Reagan's cutbacks in welfare after 1970. John Veneman left and would run unsuccessfully for lieutenant governor of California. Tom Joe left and before long joined William Copeland in his consulting firm. John Twiname was out as administrator of the SRS. He was replaced by James S. Dwight, Jr., a Weinberger protégé who had been chief deputy director of the California finance department and then an associate director for management in the OMB. James Bax resigned as commissioner of the Community Services Administration (CSA) in June 1972 and was not replaced. The CSA had a long series of acting heads.

In general, as his second term began the President appeared to be choosing department heads who would not be ardent program advocates but could be counted on to support his attempts to economize. During his first term he had enlarged and reorganized his own staff in an effort to get control of the executive branch; now he seemed to be following a different strategy, that of control through carefully calculated choices of departmental appointees. In general, he named men as under secretaries who had proved their loyalty as members of the White House staff. Simultaneously, he reduced the size of the Domestic Council, which had been set up in the first term in his Executive Office to do program planning.[7]

Along with the many changes in policy-level personnel in HEW, there was a major reorganization of the SRS. The steady subordination of program units, begun in 1967 when the SRS was created, advanced much further. The fiscal management staff continued to grow, both at headquarters and in the regions. The functions of policy control and coordination, including the preparation of regulations, were placed in the administrator's office under an associate commissioner. The commissioner's policy control staff, consisting of 8 persons on January 1, 1974, was scheduled to increase to 58 within six months, while the combined headquarters staffs of the Assistance Payments Administration, Community Services Administration, Medical Services Administration, and Rehabilitation Services Administration were to drop from 623 to 375.

The new administration's purpose was not just to change the way in which federal policy was made and administered in HEW so as to achieve greater fiscal control; more fundamentally, it was to change the character of federal-state relations. As HEW reported to the appropriations committees in 1973:

Old attitudes toward the appropriate role of the Social and Rehabilitation Service take time to change. The shift from the role of promoting major program expansion to the role of providing careful stewardship of limited resources requires major changes in attitudes. Each decision to deny Federal financial participation of inappropriate State expenditures is a painful one. The task of examining expenditures in the vast network of State and local agencies is a monumental one. It is often difficult for State agency personnel to think of the Federal Government as an active partner with a concern for the necessity of expenditures, rather than as an advocate who pays the bills without question.[8]

The SRS, this administration had declared, was no longer going to pay the bills without question. It was going to examine them first.

Through 1973 and 1974, state claims for services grants grew slowly, probably because the extreme uncertainty about federal regulations and the conflict in federal-state relations made regional officials and the state governments cautious. They were waiting for the dust to settle. Federal grants for social services in fiscal year 1974, at $1.562 billion, were only $20 million more than they had been the year before.

CHAPTER ELEVEN

Lessons

THE LESSONS most plainly to be drawn from the experience of social services grants are indisputable. The federal government should not pledge itself to unlimited monetary obligations to state governments for purposes so general as to be nearly meaningless, as it did in the services provisions of the Social Security Act. The federal executive branch should formulate grant-in-aid regulations systematically and with due concern for the financial costs and other consequences; it should state them clearly and apply them equitably. The executive branch violated all these elemental principles in this case—and violated them flagrantly, to the point of farce, with the June 17 memorandum.

Had the purpose of federal grants been clear and specific, the lack of an expenditure ceiling would not have mattered much; and had there been a limit on expenditures, the lack of purpose in the law would have mattered less than it did. It was the combination—the joining of ill-defined intentions with an unlimited obligation—that created "the worst loophole." Social services grants resembled neither general revenue sharing, for which the law fixes a spending limit, nor most categorical grant programs, whose purposes are more or less narrowly defined by statute. The plain lesson is that federal grant-in-aid laws should incorporate one or the other constraint, or both.

For all its defects, though, the law did not obligate the Department of Health, Education, and Welfare (HEW) to match whatever the states claimed as social services expenditures. Strictly speaking, federal expenditures were not "uncontrollable" in the Office of Management and Budget's (OMB's) special sense of that term. The law did not deprive the executive branch of discretion. To the contrary, the law made the executive branch bear virtually the whole burden of control.

What the federal government had to spend depended on what HEW officials permitted the states to put in their plans.*

Where legal controls governing federal expenditure are weak, administrative controls must substitute for them. Administrative controls are more necessary and, of course, more difficult to design and enforce in the absence of statutory underpinning. In this case, the Social and Rehabilitation Service (SRS) was not disposed toward control. Its initial attitude toward the states was highly permissive, its internal procedures were casual, and its capacity to develop services regulations was slight. The predictable result was gross inequity in the distribution of federal grant funds because spending responded to the individual enterprise of state governments. Here again, the lessons are plain. Given a loose law and large monetary obligations, federal grant-in-aid regulations must contain clear and equitable criteria for expenditure. They must supply what the law lacks.

There are other lessons here as well—less obvious, more open to debate, and more worthy of debate because they are the lessons drawn by the Nixon administration itself:

—That appointments to policy-level positions in the departments are crucial to presidential control. To the extent the President values fiscal control, as a practical matter he must appoint men who can be counted on to value it too, rather than program advocates or spokesmen for interests the departments serve. The President's own staff cannot be expected to compensate for deficiencies in departmental performance.

—That expenditure control cannot be adequately secured unless generalist administrators replace program specialists as policymakers for the executive branch.

Judging from the evidence of this case, the first of these two inferences is surely correct. The second is much more dubious.

The "worst loophole" was not made by designing bureaucrats who pulled wool over the eyes of hapless amateurs in the policy-level, appoint-

---

* That this particular program might have been controlled administratively of course does not indicate that the same is true of all other spending items that OMB calls uncontrollable. Some "uncontrollables" are more uncontrollable than others. Indeed, official terminology suggests relativity. OMB divides the budget into items "relatively uncontrollable under present law" and "relatively controllable outlays." If the difference between controllables and uncontrollables is a matter of degree, presumably there are also differences of degree within each classification. How much executive discretion the law allows must be judged item by item.

ive positions of HEW. Appointees—Wilbur Cohen as assistant secretary and under secretary, John Veneman as under secretary and Tom Joe as his special assistant, Mary Switzer and John Twiname as administrators of SRS, Stephen Simonds and James Bax as commissioners of the Community Services Administration (CSA)—took initiatives or made choices that, from the executive side of the government, laid the basis for turning services grants into an uncontrolled source of fiscal relief for the states. There is no reason to believe that in general they perceived that that was what they were doing. On the other hand, they had room for choice, and their choices were heavily weighted in favor of program expansion, with relatively little regard to consequences in cost or accountability in the use of federal funds.

The President's budget staff was ineffective as a check on policy-level officials in the department because its relative investment of effort in fiscal control was declining, because it lacked the foresight and knowledge to inject measures of control even when it had the opportunity to do so, as in the stage of legislative clearance, and because its opportunity to do so was limited and intermittent, being heavily dependent on legislative clearance and budget review.

It seems unlikely that the capacity of the President's staff for control or review of departmental operations can be increased significantly. The increasing preoccupation of the OMB with conceiving presidential programs responds to the President's own needs, to the preferences of the agency's staff, and thus to the agency's maintenance needs.[1] Also, there are legal and practical obstacles to engaging more deeply in reviews of operational routines in the agencies. At least since the mid-1960s, presidents have proclaimed a concern with improved management and have endorsed reorganizations of the Bureau of the Budget and the OMB to that end. The change in the budget organization's name is one sign of this new emphasis, which seems to imply a deepening involvement in the oversight of departmental routines. Early evaluations, however, suggest that results have been slight. A presidential staff of limited size and authority cannot closely scrutinize the daily conduct of a vast executive branch.[2] Even to attempt systematic review of the regulations the departments issue would overwhelm the President's office. As an avenue of review and control, the budget remains uniquely visible and accessible to the presidential staff, whose influence over the agencies will continue to be shaped by the opportunities contained in the budget review process.[3]

As agents of the President's purposes, then, departmental appointees derive their importance both from the scope of their discretion within the department and from the limited power of the President's staff. In the case described here the vagueness of the law's definitions and the open-ended authorization of expenditure magnified departmental discretion and reduced the ability of the President's staff to effect controls through the budget process. This is no doubt a special case, but its being special does not make it invalid as a test of the presidential staff's performance in reviewing departmental conduct. The very fact of its being so special is one sign of a failure in performance. Routine processes failed to prevent this seeming freak.

Within HEW, welfare administration was not organized so as to bring competing arguments between agents of fiscal control and agents of program development to the attention of appointive officials who made decisions about services grants. The CSA commissioners were unambiguously committed to program development. Fiscal considerations were to be introduced higher up, but the administration of the SRS was not organized for that purpose, at least not until 1971 when the Office of Financial Management was introduced. Most of the pressures on the SRS administrator were for expansion. It was not until the level of the secretary's office was reached that an agent of control was present and in a position to systematically counter programmatic considerations with fiscal ones, but the small size of the comptroller's office and its slowness in developing a specialized competence in departmental programs limited its ability to impose checks routinely on legislative proposals or regulations. Only when the development of the loophole reached an advanced stage did the comptroller's office begin to counter the initiatives of program units. Furthermore, in the matter of services spending even the secretary's office was by no means a mere arbiter among competing claimants. Members of that office were among the proponents of expansion in a crucial period, Tom Joe especially. The open-ended character of the services authorization invited the attention of men with an entrepreneurial disposition. Services spending was free of departmental controls partly because such controls were inherently weak and also because the opportunity embodied in the law attracted the promotionally inclined or bureaucratically ambitious.

The Nixon administration concluded that fiscal control in the SRS required a new organization as well as new men. It determined to reduce the role of the program units and to develop a fiscal management staff.

A liberal, Democratic administration of HEW had concluded in 1967 that welfare program specialists were too committed to program maintenance and therefore were incapable of innovation. Subsequently a conservative Republican administration judged them to be too committed to program maintenance and therefore profligate with public funds. Management experts, whether in the President's budget office, the department, or private consulting firms, consistently urged more generalist control; "a unified approach" was their grail and generalist administration the road to it. Hence the policymaking functions of program units in the SRS were steadily reduced after 1967, a development that was complemented at the secretarial level by the growth of the Office of the Assistant Secretary for Planning and Evaluation and above that by the increased involvement of the President's office in program planning.

In the management experts' view, professional specialization had produced rigidity, too many federal controls, and too many arbitrary limits on the choices of elected chief executives in state and local governments. And in the specific case of social services, it had not produced the desired social result, reduced dependency. They meant to change the old pattern, and in regard to services grants they really did. Reorganization broke the grip of professional social workers on administration at the federal level.

Services grants got out of control during what is apparently a transitional phase in the organization of welfare administration and perhaps of HEW generally. The transition is from the monopolization of programs by specialized, professional bureaucracies toward an administration in which generalists are in charge at least of program planning and policy formulation and perhaps also of the review of state plans and state claims for funds. It is not yet clear what the new pattern is or whether, indeed, a pattern will emerge and stabilize. It is clear only that an effort at curbing the power of the professional specialists has been under way.

Then was generalist administration somehow to blame for the debacle in social services spending? If this case is a glimpse into the administrative future of the federal system, the future could be very costly. The conclusion would be premature, however, not just because this is one case and surely idiosyncratic, but because it is not at all clear that what followed specialist control in the federal administration was generalist control. It is much easier to show that professional social workers in the Bureau of Family Services (BFS) lost control of services grants than it is to describe who or what took their place.

What followed the reorganization of 1967 was chaos. In the persistent flux of reorganization in the SRS, no organization took charge of services spending, and no clear pattern of administrative control developed following the displacement of the BFS. After 1967 responsibility for services grants was at first dispersed among SRS units, then was concentrated in the CSA, which performed ineffectually and soon lapsed, headless, into desuetude, and finally was largely taken over by a new Office of Financial Management. Meanwhile, decentralization was going on; more authority was being given to regional offices. Rather than attempt to draw inferences from the case about generalist administration, the more prudent procedure is to explore some apparent consequences of the disintegration of specialist control.

Above all, there was a decline in—one could almost say a total loss of —predictability in federal administration. Federal policies were unclear after 1967 and changed fundamentally, at first encouraging the states to use federal funds, then culminating in 1972 in efforts to close the loophole and crack down on spending. Professional specialization had implied purpose and continuity of purpose; it implied a narrow, specific, professionally derived conception of what services consisted of. Services were casework. For a generation, federal administration had followed clear, doctrinal lines of evolution in the public assistance program. Had services grants remained under the jurisdiction of the BFS, and had that bureau been permitted to perpetuate itself, services would have taken a highly predictable course: lower case loads for workers, lower supervisory ratios for casework supervisors, more professional training for workers, more elaborate individual service plans for clients, and a slow, steady reaching out for more clients.

Critics said that professional administration was resistant to innovation because it was rigidly bound by professional doctrines. This was certainly true of the BFS's administration of services grants, but such qualities, called by less pejorative names, are also highly functional in a federal system in which federal-state relations depend on developing a stable set of mutual expectations and a shared understanding among governments as to what is proper. Instability destroys federal-state comity, as the rash of law suits against HEW over services administration shows. Professional administration turned out to have had the virtues of its defects.

Second, the disintegration of specialized, professional control removed an important counterweight at the federal level to the influence of politicians. The law had created large financial opportunities, which the governors in due course discovered. It was Illinois, more than any other state, that turned social services grants into "back-door revenue sharing"; and when the Republican governor of Illinois pressed the Republican SRS administrator for an affirmative response to the state's social services plan, there was no countervailing pressure on the administrator to insist that federal funds be used for federally prescribed purposes, for there was no bureau in HEW that was capable of defining such purposes and none whose professional integrity and reputation were jeopardized by the prospect of political exploitation.

Finally, disintegration of professional control at the federal level increased the influence of politicians at the state level. Under the traditional pattern of federal-state relations in public assistance, the federal bureau focused scrutiny intensively on its state counterpart and tutored the counterpart, taking charge, so to speak, of its professional development, and supervising its administrative conduct closely. Reorganization, along with waivers of the single-state-agency requirement, broke up this relation in regard to services grants. At the state level, governors and their budget offices moved in on what had been the territory of state welfare agencies.

Federal management experts had meant to increase the power of elected chief executives and their generalist staffs at the state level, on the supposition that they would collaborate with federal counterparts in combating the parochialism and presumed tendencies to self-aggrandizement of the professional specialists. Ideally, bigger, more competent generalist staffs in state executive branches would lead to a better-planned, more efficient use of federal grant-in-aid funds. This doctrine discounted the fact that elected chief executives of state governments happen to be powerful politicians within the American party system who possess a virtually unlimited appetite for federal funds. Theoretically available to help the governors control state-agency specialists, competent generalist staffs are equally available—and are actually of great use—in helping governors to exploit the funding opportunities in federal laws.

In sum, services spending did not get out of control because the sponsoring bureau was set on aggrandizing itself. To conclude that this is what occurred would misread the case very badly. The truth is quite different: spending got out of control because the sponsoring bureau, which was professionally specialized in giving social services, lost jurisdiction, and no effective organization took its place. The vague definitions and open-ended character of the law were a necessary but insufficient condition for transforming services grants into back-door revenue sharing. The law created huge financial stakes, but then it was necessary to change the character of federal administration and of federal-state administrative relations to enable the states to capture the stakes.

If this case is at all indicative, those who would improve the conduct of American public administration in the modern welfare state should start by looking at the quality and competence of appointive officials, their conceptions of their role, the pressures that come to bear on them, and the assets they need to perform their jobs. These officials may well need protecting against the professional specialists below; but if they need help with the technocracy, it remains true, as the reformer of an earlier day believed, that they need the help of the technocracy against the politicians. Repeated announcements of the arrival of the bureaucratic, technocratic state should not obscure that fact.

Whatever techniques are used to make the professional bureaucracies responsive, it is important that the appointive officials who oversee departmental operations in HEW refrain from subjecting operating units to constant reorganization. One clear lesson of the case is that chronic reorganization exacts costs in the performance of federal administration. Federal policies were undefined and unstable partly because administrative organization was unstable, though, again, defects in the law exaggerated administrative failings. That administrative discretion was so great put a premium on administrative performance.

One approach to assisting policy-level officials is to preserve and if possible enlarge the competence that rests in two generalist organizations of long standing—the Office of General Counsel and the Office of the Comptroller. The case of social services spending gives some glimpse into the administrative resources that may be found there. In 1961 Sidney Saperstein could have designed a statute to secure strict fiscal control if that above all had been what Wilbur Cohen wanted of him. Eight years later, Joel Cohen could have helped the SRS design regula-

tions to secure fiscal restraint if that had been what Mary Switzer and
Jule Sugarman wanted. Two years after that, Cohen could have advised
John Twiname how to contain the Illinois demands if Twiname had
asked that of him. Had there been an Earl Canfield in the comptroller's
office earlier, legislative and regulatory proposals of welfare program units
would have had to undergo more careful scrutiny and would have been
more likely to encounter checks at the secretarial level. Had HEW
secretaries and under secretaries believed that there was a need for an
Earl Canfield—that is, had they felt the need for a capacity in the
comptroller's office for detailed scrutiny of welfare programs—the capacity would probably have developed sooner. The case suggests that there
is or *can* be a large reservoir of familiarity with departmental programs
and of technical skill in the budget and legal offices. Appointive officials
who learn how to enlarge and draw on this reservoir need not be at the
mercy of program units. To nurture this resource ought to be a high
priority for every administration.

How these resources of generalist competence are used depends on
how incumbent policy-level officials, both elected and appointive, choose
to use them. It depends on what goals they pursue, and with what con-
sistency and intensity of commitment. Fiscal values always compete
with other values and with a wide range of purposes—public-serving
and noble, self-interested and ignoble, or (most often) a complex blend
of the two. In a modern democracy, committed to the achievement of
large social goals and needing constantly to replenish popular gratitude,
fiscal values are very likely to be sacrificed. In the last analysis, social
services spending got out of control because incumbent administrations,
both Democratic and Republican, attached more importance to other
ends than they did to fiscal responsibility. Democratic and Republican
administrations in HEW told themselves that social services spending
was a means of helping the poor when in fact there was practically no
evidence that that purpose was being served; simply to enunciate the
purpose sanctified whatever was done. The Nixon White House ultimately was willing to pay a high price in the vain hope that this would
be of political help to a Republican governor of Illinois and would protect the public from what seemed the still higher costs that Illinois was
threatening to extract unless it was satisfied on social services.

The profligate tendencies of modern democracy will reach extremes
if laws and rules are drawn imprudently and if regularities of adminis-

trative procedure are disregarded. That is what happened here. Strengthening the executive agencies of control may slightly reduce the chances that something like it will happen again, but the procedural and organizational constraints that can be introduced through budget and financial management offices are constraints only. They affect probabilities, but they can neither alter the fundamental forces of political life nor forestall human error.

Organization of the Department of Health, Education, and Welfare, November 1971

SECRETARY; UNDER SECRETARY

OFFICE FOR CIVIL RIGHTS

ASSISTANT SECRETARY (COMMUNITY AND FIELD SERVICES)

ASSISTANT SECRETARY (LEGISLATION)

ASSISTANT SECRETARY (PLANNING AND EVALUATION)

GENERAL COUNSEL

ASSISTANT SECRETARY FOR ADMINISTRATION AND MANAGEMENT

ASSISTANT SECRETARY, COMPTROLLER

ASSISTANT SECRETARY (PUBLIC AFFAIRS)

REGIONAL OFFICES; REGIONAL DIRECTORS

ASSISTANT SECRETARY (HEALTH AND SCIENTIFIC AFFAIRS), SURGEON GENERAL

Food and Drug Administration

Office of the Commissioner
Bureau of Drugs
Bureau of Product Safety
Bureau of Veterinary Medicine
Bureau of Foods
Bureau of Radiological Health

Regional Food and Drug Directors

Health Services & Mental Health Administration

Office of the Administrator
National Center for Family Planning Services
National Center for Health Services Research and Development
National Center for Health Statistics
Center for Disease Control
National Institute of Mental Health
Health Care Facilities Service
Community Health Service
Regional Medical Programs Service
Indian Health Service
Federal Health Programs Service
Maternal and Child Health Service
Bureau of Community Environmental Management
National Institute of Occupational Safety and Health
Health Maintenance Organization Service
Comprehensive Health Planning Service

Regional Health Directors

National Institutes of Health

Office of the Director
Bureau of Health Manpower Education
National Library of Medicine
National Cancer Institute
National Eye Institute
National Heart and Lung Institute
National Institute of Allergy and Infectious Diseases
National Institute of Arthritis and Metabolic Diseases
National Institute of Child Health and Human Development
National Institute of Dental Research
National Institute of General Medical Sciences
National Institute of Neurological Diseases and Stroke
National Institute of Environmental Health Sciences
Fogarty International Center
Clinical Center
Division of Biologics Standards
Division of Computer Research and Technology
Division of Research Resources

SECRETARY; UNDER SECRETARY

SOCIAL AND REHABILITATION SERVICE

Office of the Administrator
Rehabilitation Services Administration
Community Services Administration
Administration on Aging
Medical Services Administration
Assistance Payments Administration
Youth Development and Delinquency Prevention Administration

Regional Commissioners

SOCIAL SECURITY ADMINISTRATION

Office of the Commissioner
Bureau of Data Processing
Bureau of Disability Insurance
Bureau of District Office Operations
Bureau of Health Insurance
Bureau of Hearings and Appeals
Bureau of Retirement and Survivors Insurance

Regional Commissioners

OFFICE OF EDUCATION

Office of the Commissioner
Office of Special Concerns
Deputy Commissioner for External Relations
Deputy Commissioner for Management
Office of Deputy Commissioner for School Systems
  Bureau of Adult Vocational and Technical Education
  Bureau of Education for the Handicapped
  Bureau of Elementary and Secondary Education
Office of Deputy Commissioner for Development
  Bureau of Educational Personnel Development
  Experimental Schools
  National Center for Educational Communications
  National Center for Educational Research and Development
  National Center for Educational Statistics
  Office of Program Planning and Evaluation
Office of Deputy Commissioner for Higher Education
  Bureau of Higher Education
  Bureau of Libraries and Educational Technology
  Institute of International Studies

Regional Commissioners

American Printing House for the Blind
Gallaudet College
Howard University

Organization
of the Social and Rehabilitation Service
of the Department
of Health, Education, and Welfare,
December 1971

ADMINISTRATOR; DEPUTY ADMINISTRATOR

POLICY COORDINATION STAFF

OFFICE OF PRIORITY PROGRAMS

OFFICE OF PUBLIC AFFAIRS

Division of Media Services
Division of Publications
Division of Field and Internal Information
Division of Special Projects

ASSOCIATE ADMINISTRATOR FOR PLANNING, RESEARCH, AND TRAINING

Office of Legislation

Office of Program Planning and Evaluation

Division of Program Planning
Division of Program Evaluation

Office of Manpower Development and Training

Division of Manpower Systems
Division of Standards for State/Local Agency Operations
Division of Standards for Educational Institutions

Office of Research and Demonstrations

Division of Research and Demonstrations
Division of Intramural Research
Division of Research and Training Centers
Division of International Activities

ASSOCIATE ADMINISTRATOR FOR MANAGEMENT

Office of Financial Management

Division of Budget
Division of Finance
Division of Project Grants Administration
Division of General Services

Office of Organization Development

Division of Personnel
Division of Methods and Manpower Utilization

Office of Program Statistics and Data Systems

National Center for Social Statistics
Division of State Systems Management
Division of Internal Systems and Report Development
Division of Forecasting and Trend Analysis
Division of Data Processing

ADMINISTRATION ON AGING

Office of the Commissioner
Division of Information
Division of Administration
Division of Program and Legislative Analysis
Division of Older Americans Service
Division of Research, Demonstration and Training

ASSISTANCE PAYMENTS ADMINISTRATION

Office of the Commissioner
Division of Program Payment Standards
Division of State Administrative and Fiscal Standards
Division of Program Evaluation

ADMINISTRATOR; DEPUTY ADMINISTRATOR

COMMUNITY SERVICES ADMINISTRATION

Office of the Commissioner
  Executive Office
  Public Affairs Staff
Office of Planning and Evaluation
Office of Service Delivery
Office of Field Support Services and State Management Services
Office of Program Management
  Common Services Staff
Division of Child and Family Services
Division of Services to the Aged and Handicapped
Division of Self-Support Programs

MEDICAL SERVICES ADMINISTRATION

Office of the Commissioner
Office of Program Planning and Evaluation
Office of Program Innovation
Division of Management Information and Payment Systems
Division of Program Operations and Standards
Division of Technical Assistance and Training

REHABILITATION SERVICES ADMINISTRATION

Office of the Commissioner
Office of Planning and Policy Development
Office of the Blind and Visually Handicapped
Office for Deafness and Communicative Disorders
Division of Special Populations
Division of Developmental Disabilities
Division of Service Systems
Division of Manpower Development
Division of Planning and Management Assistance
Division of Monitoring and Program Analysis
Division of State Program Financial Operations
Division of Budget

YOUTH DEVELOPMENT AND DELINQUENCY PREVENTION ADMINISTRATION

Office of the Commissioner
Division of Administrative Management
Division of Program Development

ASSOCIATE ADMINISTRATOR FOR FIELD OPERATIONS

Cuban Refugee Program

Office of the Director
Cuban Refugee Emergency Center, Miami, Florida

Regional Offices; Regional Commissioners

Notes

MUCH OF THIS STUDY has been based on information obtained during interviews with approximately forty-five persons, including most of the leading participants. In many cases, however, my sources asked to remain anonymous; therefore, a number of the quotations used in my account have not been attributed. In some instances, I also have cited official documents without identifying their location in archives or agency files. Copies of these documents, which were obtained from official sources, are in my files.

CHAPTER ONE

1. *The Budget of the United States Government, Fiscal Year 1975* (1974), pp. 318–19. For a definition of uncontrollability, see Murray Weidenbaum, "On the Effectiveness of Congressional Control of the Public Purse," *National Tax Journal*, vol. 18 (December 1965), pp. 370–74. Revised versions appear in Robert H. Haveman and Julius Margolis, eds., *Public Expenditures and Policy Analysis* (Markham 1970); and in *The Analysis and Evaluation of Public Expenditures: The PPB System*, A Compendium of Papers Submitted to the Subcommittee on Economy in Government of the Joint Economic Committee, 91 Cong. 1 sess. (1969), vol. 1, pp. 357–68.

2. *The Budget of the United States Government, Fiscal Year 1975*, p. 3.

3. See *Improving Congressional Control of the Budget*, Hearings before the Subcommittee on Budgeting, Management, and Expenditures of the Senate Committee on Government Operations, 93 Cong. 1 sess. (1973); *Improving Congressional Control over the Budget*, compiled by the staff of the Subcommittee on Budgeting, Management, and Expenditures for the Senate Committee on Government Operations, 93 Cong. 1 sess. (1973); American Enterprise Institute for Public Policy Research, *Can Congress Control Spending?* (Washington, D.C.: AEI, 1973); and Aaron Wildavsky, "The Annual Expenditure Increment—or How Congress Can Regain Control of the Budget," *The Public Interest*, Fall 1973, pp. 84–108.

4. Touche Ross and Co., "Cost Analysis of Social Services, Fiscal Year 1972" (February 2, 1973; processed), p. 64.

5. *Staff Data with Respect to Limiting Federal Funds for Social Services*, prepared for the Senate Finance Committee, 92 Cong. 2 sess. (1972), p. 4.

6. *Congressional Record*, vol. 118, pt. 27, 92 Cong. 2 sess. (1972), p. 35518.

7. *Having the Power, We Have the Duty*, Report of the Advisory Council on Public Welfare to the Secretary of Health, Education, and Welfare (June 1966), p. 47. The official position was stated as early as 1948 in the *Annual Report of the Federal Security Administration* for that year, which said (p. 193): "To help families remain together and to enable families and adults to become self-supporting, to make fuller use of community resources, or to solve individual or family problems, the Social Security Administration advocates the extension of Federal financial participation to cover all welfare services administered by the staff of the public welfare agency. The Administration believes that comprehensive welfare services should in time be available to persons requesting them—whether needy or not—in all communities of the Nation."

8. Nixon-Agnew Campaign Committee, *Nixon on the Issues* (1968), p. 128.

9. Daniel P. Moynihan, *The Politics of a Guaranteed Income: The Nixon Administration and the Family Assistance Plan* (Random House, 1973), p. 108.

CHAPTER TWO

1. *Open-Ended Federal Matching of State Social Service Expenditure Authorized under the Public Assistance Titles of the Social Security Act*, Hearings before the Subcommittee on Fiscal Policy of the Joint Economic Committee, 92 Cong. 2 sess. (1972), p. 3.

2. Memorandum for the President, November 1, 1962 (President's Office Files, HEW 1961, John F. Kennedy Archives, Waltham, Mass.). For background on the legislation, see Charles E. Gilbert, "Policy-Making in Public Welfare," *Political Science Quarterly*, vol. 81 (June 1966), pp. 196–224; Gilbert Y. Steiner, *Social Insecurity: The Politics of Welfare* (Rand McNally, 1966), pp. 34–47; and Martha Derthick, *The Influence of Federal Grants: Public Assistance in Massachusetts* (Harvard University Press, 1970), pp. 129–33.

3. 76 Stat. 172. An official summary of the contents is contained in Wilbur J. Cohen and Robert M. Ball, "Public Welfare Amendments of 1962 and Proposals for Health Insurance for the Aged," *Social Security Bulletin*, October 1962, pp. 3–16.

4. Social Security Act, Sec. 403(a)(3)(E) and Sec. 1603(a)(4)(E), *Compilation of the Social Security Laws*, H. Doc. 616, 87 Cong. 2 sess. (1963), pp. 136, 213.

5. *Public Welfare Amendments of 1962*, Hearings before the House Ways and Means Committee, 87 Cong. 2 sess. (1962), pp. 452–58.

6. Kathryn B. Goodwin to William L. Mitchell, commissioner of social security, "Provision for Services to Non-Recipients in Public Welfare Bill" (microfilm roll 46, HEW, John F. Kennedy Archives). The date of this memorandum is illegible but is circa January 18, 1962. The same memorandum stated that "costs can be substantially controlled for both recipients and non-recipients by the scope of services prescribed by the Secretary for these groups." Director Goodwin added, "We never considered that the costs of services for non-recipients would be very great. The required and recommended services for recipients would leave little manpower or funds to put into non-recipient services for some years."

7. *Public Welfare Amendments of 1962*, H. Rept. 1414, 87 Cong. 2 sess. (1962), p. 11; and *Public Welfare Amendments of 1962*, S. Rept. 1589, 87 Cong. 2 sess. (1962), p. 8. The statute also provided that purchased services should be ones "which in the judgment of the State agency cannot be as effectively provided by the staff of such State or local agency and are not otherwise reasonably available to individuals in need of them."

8. Memorandum, Sidney Saperstein to "AWW" (Alanson W. Willcox), December 6, 1961, "Considerations and Reservations in Connection with the Public Welfare Bill" (file P.L. 543, 87 Cong., no. 7, Office of Assistant General Counsel for Legislation, HEW).

9. *Congressional Record*, vol. 118, pt. 27, 92 Cong. 2 sess. (1972), p. 35517.

10. *Open-Ended Federal Matching*, Hearings, p. 13.

11. Social Security Act, Sec. (403)(a)(3)(A)(iii) and Sec. 1603(a)(4)(A)(iii), *Compilation of the Social Security Laws*, pp. 135, 212.

12. Sec. 4242.1, pt. 4, "Handbook of Public Assistance Administration," transmitted by BFS State Letter 606 (November 30, 1962; processed).

13. *Public Assistance Act of 1962*, Hearings before the Senate Finance Committee, 87 Cong. 2 sess. (1962), pp. 63–64.

14. 81 Stat. 821; and Social Security Act, Sec. 406(d), *Compilation of the Social Security Laws*, vol. 1, H. Doc. 93-117, 93 Cong. 1 sess. (1973), p. 206.

15. *Social Security Amendments of 1967*, S. Rept. 744, 90 Cong. 1 sess. (1967), p. 157.

CHAPTER THREE

1. *Federal Register*, vol. 34, no. 17 (January 25, 1969), pp. 1243–44; and no. 18 (January 28, 1969), pp. 1354–63. An interim version appeared in the *Federal Register*, vol. 33, no. 138 (July 17, 1968), pp. 10234–39. Regulations governing the public assistance programs administered by the SRS constitute Chapter II, Title 45, *Code of Federal Regulations* (1973).

2. Press release, Office of the Secretary, Department of Health, Education, and Welfare, August 15, 1967. Much of this release appears in the *Congressional Record*, vol. 113, pt. 17, 90 Cong. 1 sess. (1967), pp. 22607–08.

3. I am indebted to Pauline Milius, a research assistant in the Brookings Governmental Studies program, for valuable background papers on the reorganization.

4. Memorandum, Jule M. Sugarman to Mary E. Switzer, "Organization of the Children's Bureau," December 26, 1968 (Sugarman's office file, Record Group 235, National Archives).

5. This distinction and related developments, including the reorganization of 1967 and the organizational separation of services and income maintenance, were adumbrated by the report of a Task Force on Social Services submitted to HEW Assistant Secretary Lisle C. Carter, Jr., on September 1, 1966. Part of the task force, consisting of members from outside the department, favored creating a new Social Services Administration wholly separate from the administration of public assistance and designed to facilitate state and regional diversity in administering social service. Ellen Winston, commissioner of the Welfare Administration, reacted sharply to the report and discouraged its circulation. She argued for keeping services within the Welfare Administration (perhaps to be called by some other name) on the ground that programs should be pulled together rather than fragmented further. The reorganization of 1967 did both some pulling together (of HEW bureaus under a new umbrella agency) and some fragmenting (by removing responsibility for services grants from the BFS and distributing it among several subunits of the SRS).

6. Sec. 4281, "Handbook of Public Assistance Administration," transmitted by BFS State Letter 606 (November 30, 1962; processed).

7. Letter, John J. Hurley to J. M. Wedemeyer, January 3, 1966 (Calif. SS-15, Acc. No. 363-73-8, R.G. 363, Washington National Records Center, Suitland, Md.). Boxes 22 and 23 of this accession contain BFS documents on the California preschool compensatory program. The federal review, completed in 1968, commended state officials for "vision and foresight" and found that the cooperating departments had "developed a high quality preschool program . . . through a sound administrative structure. . . ." It also found, however, that "reporting from the project does not adequately provide a regular flow of accurate program data for purposes of program development, evaluation and fiscal control." (U.S. Department of Health, Education, and Welfare, Social and Rehabilitation Service, "California State Preschool Program: Study of the Interagency Agreement Between the State Departments of Social Welfare and Education for the Purchase of Preschool Education Under the AFDC Program" [August 1968; processed], pp. 1–2.)

8. Sec. 226.1(a)(5), Chapter 2, Title 45, *Code of Federal Regulations* (1971), p. 55.

9. For a detailed statement of the bureau's objectives and an account of how it pursued them in one state, Massachusetts, see Martha Derthick, *The Influence of Federal Grants: Public Assistance in Massachusetts* (Harvard University Press, 1970).

10. Use of this format for public assistance regulations was new. The BPA/FS had used a system of state letters, which were consolidated and codified in the "Handbook of Public Assistance Administration." The change to the *Federal Register* was itself a response to the increasing politicization of public assistance. At least technically, regulations were a more open procedure, entailing preliminary publication in the *Register* and solicitation of comments. The change in turn furthered erosion of the old regulatory and hortatory stance. The "Handbook" had grown fat and failed to distinguish clearly between what was required of the states and what was merely hoped for. Adopting the more legalistic form of guidance compelled the SRS to consider carefully what it was actually willing to enforce, a process that thinned out the rules.

11. For a representative critique, see *Poverty Amid Plenty: The American Paradox*, The Report of the President's Commission on Income Maintenance Programs (1969), pp. 138–40.

CHAPTER FOUR

1. Daniel P. Moynihan, *The Politics of a Guaranteed Income: The Nixon Administration and the Family Assistance Plan* (Random House, 1973), p. 444.

2. Interview, March 20, 1974; and U.S. Department of Health, Education, and Welfare, Social and Rehabilitation Service, *Financing Rehabilitation Services* (1969), pp. 7–8. For another statement by Copeland, see "New Budget Approaches for State Governments," *Appalachia*, September 1970, pp. 19–23. *Appalachia* is published by the Appalachian Regional Commission, and the article contained Copeland's advice to Appalachian state governments about how to exploit services funds.

3. For example, see Harold Seidman, *Politics, Position, and Power: The Dynamics of Federal Organization* (Oxford University Press, 1970), chap. 5.

CHAPTER FIVE

1. Unpublished data from HEW.

2. In addition to interviews, this information on California was drawn from California Legislature, Senate Interim Committee on Social Welfare, *A Study of Welfare Expenditures (Public Social Service)*, Report of the Subcommittee of General Research (Sacramento, 1969); California Legis-

lature, "California Welfare: A Legislative Program for Reform," A Staff Report to the Assembly Committee on Social Welfare by Assembly Office of Research and Staff of the Assembly Committee on Social Welfare (Sacramento, February 1969; processed); and U.S. Department of Health, Education, and Welfare, Social and Rehabilitation Service, "California State Preschool Program: Study of the Interagency Agreement between the State Departments of Social Welfare and Education for the Purchase of Preschool Education Under the AFDC Program" (August 1968; processed).

3. "California Welfare," p. 269.

4. Comptroller General of the United States, *Some Problems in Contracting for Federally Assisted Child Care Services*, Report to the Congress, B-164031(3) (June 13, 1973), p. 11.

5. According to a state legislative report, in four years (California's fiscal year 1963–64 to 1967–68), the federal share of the cost of protective services in the state rose from 8.2 percent to 65.5 percent. Federal grants rose from $4 million to $130 million, state funds from $34 million to $54 million, and local funds from $12.5 million to $15 million. The report defined protective services as family and children's services and adoptions, day-care services, protective services for the mentally handicapped, maternal and child health, crippled children's services, the preschool education program, children's centers, and compensatory education projects. These figures cannot be taken as a reliable indicator of the impact of services grants, however, since other sources of federal support (e.g., the Economic Opportunity Act, Title I of the Elementary and Secondary Education Act, and the child welfare sections of the Social Security Act) contributed substantially. (*A Study of Welfare Expenditures*, p. 26.)

6. "California Welfare," pp. 216–18.

7. Ibid., pp. 255–56. It is possible that the arrangement described here would not have qualified for federal matching funds. Federal regulations stipulated that donated private funds could not revert to the donor's facility or use.

CHAPTER SIX

1. Tom Joe, "Finding Welfare Dollars," Supplement 3: "Public Welfare—Challenge to Validity" (prepared by the Technical Assistance Project, American Public Welfare Association, February 1968; processed), pp. 1, 2, 17. After leaving HEW, Joe joined McKinsey and Company, a New York-based management consulting firm, for nine months, and then Copeland Associates, Copeland's consulting firm. There are biographical sketches of Joe in *National Journal*, June 17, 1972, p. 1013; and in Vincent J. and Vee Burke, *Nixon's Good Deed: Welfare Reform* (Columbia University Press, 1974), pp. 50–51.

2. *Departments of Labor and Health, Education, and Welfare Appropriations for 1971*, Hearings before the House Appropriations Committee, 91 Cong. 1 sess. (1970), pt. 4, p. 2.

3. Ibid., p. 3.

4. *Congressional Record*, vol. 115, pt. 21, 91 Cong. 1 sess. (1969), p. 28195; and H.R. 16311, *The Family Assistance Act of 1970*, Revised and resubmitted to the Senate Committee on Finance by the Administration, 91 Cong. 2 sess. (1970), pp. 87–116.

5. "Statement by Secretary Robert H. Finch Announcing Submission of Proposals to Reform the Human Service Program of the Department of Health, Education, and Welfare, June 18, 1970," *Weekly Compilation of Presidential Documents* (June 20, 1970), pp. 786–87.

6. *National Journal*, September 5, 1970, pp. 1905–15, especially p. 1914.

7. The HEW member, Robert E. Patricelli, was deputy assistant secretary for planning and evaluation from May 1969 until April 1970, when he was named to the newly created position of deputy under secretary for policy. His oversight of services planning began when he was in the former position.

8. Memorandum to Lewis H. Butler and Frederic V. Malek, March 11, 1970 (Box 10, Acc. No. 72A-5013, R.G., 363, Washington National Records Center, Suitland, Md.). This memo appears not to have been sent.

9. *National Journal*, September 19, 1970, pp. 2049–51.

10. *National Journal*, March 3, 1973, pp. 305–11; and Rufus E. Miles, Jr., *The Department of Health, Education, and Welfare* (Praeger, 1974), pp. 59–61.

11. For illustrations of what Pennsylvania did to enlarge its services funding and what consultants advised the state to do, see Rocco D'Amico and Seldon P. Todd, "Financing Human Service Programs" (Minneapolis: Institute for Interdisciplinary Studies, American Rehabilitation Foundation, May 1970; processed), pp. 68–104. With the papers by Copeland (see note 2, chap. 4) and Joe (see note 1), this report constitutes the how-to-do-it literature for states on services funding. It justly credits Joe with being "the first person to attempt to set forth the major concepts as related to funding potential that are embodied in the 1967 Amendments" (p. 105).

12. Oral deposition of Theodore Levine, August 2, 1973 (*Mason* v. *DeGeorge*, 73-436-N, USDC, Md.), transcript, pp. 14–16.

CHAPTER SEVEN

1. *U.S. News and World Report*, February 8, 1971, p. 3; for extended coverage of welfare spending, see also the issues for September 5, 1969, pp. 28–29; November 30, 1970, pp. 32–35; June 7, 1971, pp. 59–61; and August 9, 1971, pp. 13–16.

2. For a superb recapitulation of the political situation of the Ogilvie administration and how that administration performed budget planning, see "Some Reflections on PPBS in Illinois State Government: A Statement by the Deputy Director [Cotton], October 1971," in Illinois Bureau of the Budget, *Papers in Public Finance: The Ogilvie Years* (no date, circa 1973), pp. 127–34.

3. "The Budget Message: Richard B. Ogilvie to the 77th General Assembly, March 3, 1971," ibid., pp. 113–20, especially p. 115.

4. What was going for day care, however, was not necessarily being used, as Congress had intended, for the children of public assistance recipients or other poor people who were working or were in training for work. In 1973 a report of the comptroller general concluded, on the basis of surveys in California and Pennsylvania: "The low use of services by Work Incentive Program participants and the relatively large number of program enrollees whose parents were not working or training raise serious questions as to whether child-care services achieve the primary objective of the program . . . to help welfare families become self-sufficient." (Comptroller General of the United States, *Some Problems in Contracting for Federally Assisted Child-Care Services*, Report to the Congress, B-164031(3) [June 13, 1973], pp. 1–2.)

5. Booz, Allen Public Administration Services, Inc., "Purchase of Social Service: Study of the Experience of Three States in Purchase of Service by Contract under the Provisions of the 1967 Amendments to the Social Security Act" (U.S. Department of Health, Education, and Welfare, Social and Rehabilitation Service, January 29, 1971), pp. 13–14 (U.S. Department of Commerce, National Technical Information Service, PB 197 582).

6. Letter, Harold O. Swank to Donald F. Simpson, December 30, 1970. The Illinois proposals were set forth in three separate communications from Swank to Simpson on this date. Copies were supplied to me. I have not seen either the files of the Illinois Department of Public Aid or those of the SRS regional office in Chicago.

7. *Chicago Tribune*, February 11, 1971.

8. Deposition of James A. Bax, July 27, 1973 (*Mason v. DeGeorge*, 73-436-N, USDC, Md.), transcript, pp. 30–31.

9. According to the executive office of the CSA, Bax took office on June 13, 1971. Bax testified in 1973 that the "June 17th memorandum . . . was put out by an individual, Stephen Simonds, who was actually no longer Commissioner of CSA when he attached his name to it. Of course, on that date, June 17th, I was then Commissioner." (Ibid., p. 16.) Simonds stayed in Washington for two or three weeks to help his successor get oriented. He signed the memorandum in that period. A source in HEW pointed out that for Bax to have signed the memorandum might have created the appearance of impropriety. In his previous position in Florida, he had negotiated several services arrangements with the SRS. It would have been unseemly for him, as one of his first acts as CSA commissioner,

to issue a document that confirmed the validity of actions he had previously taken in the state.

10. Memorandum, Stephen P. Simonds to regional commissioners, SRS, "Clarification of Policies on the Purchase of Social Services from Other Public Agencies," June 17, 1971.

11. See Peter E. Sitkin, "Welfare Law: Narrowing the Gap Between Congressional Policy and Local Practice," in Joint Economic Committee, *Studies in Public Welfare*, Paper 5, pt. 2: *Issues in Welfare Administration: Intergovernmental Relationships*, 92 Cong. 2 sess. (1972), pp. 36–68: and *National Journal*, February 20, 1971, pp. 401–09.

12. The brief is in the form of a letter from Charles A. Miller, a member of Covington and Burling, to Twiname, May 27, 1971.

13. It is interesting to compare the June 17 memorandum with memorandums of legal advice prepared more or less contemporaneously by the Office of the General Counsel. The following, for example, after disposing of a question about the definition of a "child-care institution" under the foster-care section of the AFDC statute (Title IV-A of the Social Security Act), proceeded to take a tough, clear stand on the permissible uses of services funds:

. . . we would point out that the Title IV-A programs of assistance and services are basically programs for helping families living together as a unit. Insofar as there is authority for Federal matching of assistance or services to persons not living with their family, it is only in narrowly-defined exceptional circumstances. . . . We do not believe that Title IV-A was intended to provide institutional care on a general basis as a service, or to include persons residing in a particular type of institution as potential recipients on the basis of their residence in that institution. . . .

What is now proposed by States such as Florida and Oregon is to add services in their child-care institutions and to claim that the institutional living arrangements are secondary to the services, and not vice-versa. This does not ring true, and acceptance of any such scheme for Federal matching would in our view amount to a major change in policy, a major change in point of view of what is includable as services under present law, and a cost factor which might have effects in the hundreds of millions of dollars. We believe that any such change should come by Congressional, not administrative, action. And if done administratively, it should at least involve full consideration by the Administrator and Secretary.

For this reason, we cannot give legal clearance to any of the proposals to help States to try to make their child-care institutional costs qualify for Federal matching as services. This is just circumvention of existing Federal policy. The States should be told that current Federal law doesn't allow what they're trying to do. If it is believed that the present regulations appear superficially to countenance this kind of distortion, the regulations should be clarified and narrowed in scope.

(Elizabeth A. Croog to J. Louis Browning, CSA, "Oregon—Youth Care Centers—Availability of Federal Funds," March 8, 1971.)

14. James A. Bax to regional commissioners, SRS, "Clarification of Policies on the Purchase of Social Services from Other Public Agencies," July 14, 1971.

15. "Description of Revisions in Illinois Welfare Program, October 5, 1971," *Papers in Public Finance*, pp. 135–46.

16. Both stories are on p. 1 of the *Tribune*, November 3, 1971.

17. *Congressional Record*, vol. 117, pt. 32, 92 Cong. 1 sess. (1971), pp. 41737–57, especially p. 41756. See also the perceptive editorial in the *Washington Post*, November 21, 1971, and the news story in the *New York Times*, November 18, 1971. Much of the understanding between Senator Percy and the Nixon administration is in the public record.

18. *National Journal*, December 11, 1971, p. 2451.

19. Memorandum, James A. Bax to William J. Page, Jr., "Requests (4) for Waivers of the Single State Agency Requirement—Illinois," December 20, 1971. The memorandum was drafted by J. Louis Browning, policy coordinator and field liaison officer in the CSA, who was a veteran career official with many years of experience in the BFS. Browning later recalled that Bax had never failed to sign anything that Browning had put before him. His subsequent actions, however, might or might not be consistent with what he had signed.

20. Memorandum, Thomas Laughlin, Jr., to William J. Page, Jr., November 21, 1971.

21. Memorandum, Joel Cohen to John D. Twiname, "Intergovernmental Cooperation Act—Waiver of Single State Agency—Retroactive Effect," February 4, 1972.

22. Bax deposition, p. 32.

23. See *The Budget of the United States Government, Fiscal Year 1973* (1972), app., p. 451.

24. "Article Written by Richard B. Ogilvie Appearing in Perspective, Chicago Tribune, December 31, 1972," *Papers in Public Finance*, pp. 362–65.

25. "Some Reflections on PPBS," p. 130.

CHAPTER EIGHT

1. The SRS regional commisioner in Seattle wrote as follows to state welfare departments:

We want to call to your attention again the Community Services Administration memorandum dated June 17, 1971, "Clarification of Policies on the Purchase of Social Services from Other Public Agencies," recently released to your agency by Regional Office staff.

Your review of these policies, I am sure, has indicated to you that the thrust of this policy development is to greatly expand social service funding for Family and Children's Services and Adult Service Programs. We encourage you and your planning staff to take full advantage of these more liberal interpretations of the availability of Federal Financial Participation in social services funding to States. . . .

We are looking forward to working with you on expansion of needed social service programs for our clientele. . . .

(Richard A. Grant to Sidney E. Smith, Department of Social and Health Services, Washington State, August 17, 1971.) This letter, however, also called attention to the need to use federal funds to supplement and expand social services rather than to replace current state and local expenditures.

2. Bax to regional commissioners, SRS, August 11, 1971 (Box 18, Acc. No. 363-73-8, Washington National Records Center, Suitland, Md.).

3. *New York Times*, June 8, 1972; and *National Journal*, June 17, 1972, pp. 1007–14.

4. The authoritative source of expenditure data, by states, is the so-called blue book of SRS, issued for each fiscal year as "State Expenditures for Public Assistance Programs Approved under Titles I, IV-A, X, XIV, XVI, and XIX of the Social Security Act."

5. Touche Ross and Co., "Cost Analysis of Social Services, Fiscal Year 1972" (February 2, 1973; processed), pp. 2–8. Evidence bearing on this point has been gathered also by Robert Caulk, a candidate for a Ph.D. degree at the Florence Heller School of Brandeis University. Caulk's dissertation was not available at the time of my research, but he described his findings in a letter, October 15, 1974: "I investigated state funding of social services in California, Illinois, and New York. The data I collected in those states were not conclusive; yet by describing the planning processes and the Federal response to increases in claims between fiscal 1971 through 1973, I feel that a fairly strong evidentiary case has been made which indicates that tremendous increases in Federal expenditures for social services represent substitution of Federal dollars for state funds previously committed to support traditionally funded social services."

6. *Departments of Labor and Health, Education, and Welfare Appropriations for 1973*, Hearings before a Subcommittee of the House Committee on Appropriations, 92 Cong. 2 sess. (1972), pp. 225–26.

7. *National Journal*, June 17, 1972, p. 1013.

8. *National Journal*, August 12, 1972, p. 1300. My summary of the memorandum is based also on a reading of the full document.

9. *Message from the President of the United States Vetoing H.R. 15417, An Act Making Appropriations for the Departments of Labor, and Health, Education, and Welfare, and Related Agencies, for the Fiscal Year Ending June 30, 1973, and for Other Purposes*, H. Doc. 92-343, 92 Cong. 2 sess. (1972), p. 3.

10. These stories appear in the *Congressional Record*, vol. 118, pt. 21, 92 Cong. 2 sess. (1972), pp. 27436–40; and pt. 22, pp. 28696–97.

11. *Open-Ended Federal Matching of State Social Service Expenditure Authorized under the Public Assistance Titles of the Social Security Act*, Hearings before the Subcommittee on Fiscal Policy of the Joint Economic Committee, 92 Cong. 2 sess. (1972).

12. See especially *Revenue Sharing*, Hearing before the Senate Finance Committee, 92 Cong. 2 sess. (1972), pp. 111–12, 135–38.

13. 86 Stat. 945–47. The cap on social services grants is Title III. The

congressional politics of this action is reported in *National Journal*, October 7, 1972, pp. 1562–66.

CHAPTER NINE

1. "Legislative Coordination and Clearance," OMB Circular A-19, rev. (July 31, 1972; processed).
2. Cohen's notes and Saperstein's draft are in file P.L. 543, 87 Cong. (H.R. 10606), no. 6, Office of the Assistant General Counsel for Legislation, HEW.
3. Memorandum, Reginald G. Conley to Alanson W. Willcox, "October 24 Meeting with Budget Bureau Staff on Welfare Legislative Program," October 25, 1961, ibid.
4. File R3-8/62.1, 87-HR 10606 PL 543, Bureau of the Budget; HEW microfilm roll no. 45, John F. Kennedy Library, Waltham, Mass.
5. Elmer W. Smith to Edwin H. Yourman, "Services Eligible for 75% Matching under the 1962 Public Welfare Amendments," October 29, 1965 (in file "School Dropouts—Staff Development," 1963–1967, Acc. No. 72A6755, R.G. 363, Box 16, Washington National Records Center, Suitland, Md.).
6. Joel Cohen to Ellen Winston, "Public Assistance Programs—75% Matching for Training and Services—Extent of Authority," November 5, 1965, ibid.
7. Because the OMB's legislative files are closed for ten years, I have not seen the file on the 1967 amendments.
8. Memorandum by W. Howard Tucker, "Possible Questions for FY '72 Budget Hearings," October 19, 1970 (CSA budget files, Acc. No. 363-73-8, R.G. 363, Box 18, Washington National Records Center).
9. Phillip S. Hughes, recorded interview by Larry J. Hackman, April 24, 1968 (transcript, p. 9, John F. Kennedy Library).
10. *Departments of Labor, and Health, Education, and Welfare Appropriations, Fiscal Year 1971*, Hearings before the Senate Committee on Appropriations, 91 Cong. 2 sess. (1970), pt. 4, pp. 1941–43.
11. Ibid., pt. 6, pp. 3872–73.
12. *Departments of Labor and Health, Education, and Welfare and Related Agencies Appropriations, Fiscal Year 1972*, Hearings before the Senate Appropriations Committee, 92 Cong. 1 sess. (1971), pt. 2, p. 1112.
13. The House Appropriations Committee explained its reaction to the proposed 110 percent ceiling as follows in 1970: "Many of the State welfare agencies have expressed opposition to this provision. The committee has not included it in the bill, because by fixing a rigid ceiling on each State based on a percentage of 1970 expenditures it appears to discriminate unfairly against those States which have been slow in developing their programs but are now ready to expand them." (*Departments of Labor, and*

Health, Education, and Welfare, and Related Agencies Appropriations Bill, 1971, H. Rept. 91-1310, 91 Cong. 2 sess. [1970], p. 34.) For the Senate debates, see *Congressional Record*, vol. 116, pt. 28, 91 Cong. 2 sess. (1970), pp. 38299–306; and vol. 117, pt. 21, 92 Cong. 1 sess. (1971), pp. 23213–26.

14. Booz, Allen Public Administration Services, Inc., "Purchase of Social Service: Study of Experience of Three States in Purchase of Service by Contract under the Provisions of the 1967 Amendments to the Social Security Act" (U.S. Department of Health, Education, and Welfare, Social and Rehabilitation Service, January 29, 1971), 163 pp. (U.S. Department of Commerce, National Technical Information Service, PB 197 582).

15. *United States Government Organization Manual, 1972/73* (1972), p. 213.

16. For a participant's appraisal of PPBS in HEW, see Alice M. Rivlin, "The Planning, Programing, and Budgeting System in the Department of Health, Education, and Welfare: Some Lessons from Experience," in *The Analysis and Evaluation of Public Expenditures: The PPB System,* A compendium of papers submitted to the Subcommittee on Economy in Government of the Joint Economic Committee, 91 Cong. 1 sess. (1969), vol. 3, pt. 5 (Brookings Reprint 162).

17. Touche Ross and Co., "Cost Analysis of Social Services, Fiscal Year 1972" (February 2, 1973; processed).

18. From a report by Harbridge House, Inc., to the SRS, November 30, 1967, p. 2 of an enclosure to letter, Elmer N. Engstrom to Mary Switzer.

19. *Second Supplemental Appropriation Bill,* 1972, Hearings before the Subcommittees of the House Appropriations Committee, 92 Cong. 2 sess. (1972), p. 630.

20. U.S. Department of Health, Education, and Welfare, Social and Rehabilitation Service, Office of Financial Management, "Statement of Functions: Division of State Grants Administration," attachment to "A Plan for Improved Federal and State Management of Public Assistance Programs" (February 1972; processed).

21. Administrator, SRS, to regional commissioners, "Interpretation of Federal Regulations in Determining the Allowability of State Claims for Federal Financial Participation in Expenditures for Social Services, December 20, 1972.

CHAPTER TEN

1. *The States of Florida, Tallahassee, Florida . . . and Virginia, Richmond, Virginia v. Weinberger and others,* 2173-73 (USDC, District of Columbia, December 13, 1973).

2. On the issue of retroactive claims, see *Wall Street Journal*, July 23, 1973.

3. *Social Security Amendments of 1972*, S. Rept. 92-1230, 92 Cong. 2 sess. (1972), p. 108. The conference report on the revenue-sharing bill is *State and Local Fiscal Assistance Act of 1972*, H. Rept. 92-1450, 92 Cong. 2 sess. (1972), p. 35.

4. *Second Supplemental Appropriation Bill, 1973*, Hearings before Subcommittees of the House Committee on Appropriations, 93 Cong. 1 sess. (1973), pt. 1, p. 811. On the floor in 1972 Michel had denounced the loophole, but in 1970 in committee he had opposed the administration's proposal for closing it. Michel was the ranking Republican on the subcommittee that handled HEW appropriations. (See *National Journal*, June 17, 1972, p. 1011.)

5. The complicated story of this executive-legislative dispute may be traced in the *Federal Register*, vol. 38 (February 16, 1973), pp. 4608-13; May 1, 1973, pp. 10781–88; June 1, 1973, pp. 14375–76; September 10, 1973, pp. 24872–74; and October 31, 1973, pp. 30072–78; *Social and Rehabilitation Services*, Hearing before the Select Subcommittee on Education of the House Education and Labor Committee, 93 Cong. 1 sess. (1973); *Social Services Regulations*, Hearings before the Senate Finance Committee, 93 Cong. 1 sess., 2 pts. (1973); and *National Journal Reports*, August 4, 1973, pp. 1132–37, and November 17, 1973, p. 1731.

6. The new legislation is P.L. 93-637, the Social Services Amendments of 1974, which constitute Title XX of the Social Security Act.

7. For analyses of this strategy, see *National Journal*, March 10, 1973, pp. 329–40; and Richard P. Nathan, *The Plot that Failed: Nixon and the Administrative Presidency* (Wiley, 1975).

8. U.S. Department of Health, Education, and Welfare, Social and Rehabilitation Service, "Improved Federal and State Management of Public Assistance Programs, A Report to the Committees on Appropriations, United States Senate and House of Representatives" (March 1973; processed), p. 1.

CHAPTER ELEVEN

1. See Allen Schick, "The Budget Bureau That Was: Thoughts on the Rise, Decline, and Future of a Presidential Agency," *Law and Contemporary Problems*, vol. 35 (Summer 1970), pp. 519–39 (Brookings Reprint 213). In 1967 a self-study by the bureau concluded that examiners believed "development of new policies and programs" to be their single most important activity—more important than budget review and analysis, program review and analysis, coordination of current programs, and five other categories. They spent more time on budget review and analysis than on the development of new policies and programs, but this was a source of dis-

satisfaction. They would have liked to increase the proportion spent on the latter. Of course, this survey was taken at a time when program innovation had been proceeding at a rapid pace. Perhaps a similar survey five years later would have yielded different results. (U.S. Bureau of the Budget, "Initial Paper on Organizing and Relating the Budget Bureau's Activities in the Sixties and Seventies: The Divisions and the Offices," in "The Work of the Steering Group on Evaluation of the Bureau of the Budget," 3 vols. [February–July 1967; processed], OMB library, Washington, D.C.)

2. David Halberstam reported an illustrative incident from the field of military affairs. Early in the Vietnam war the Kennedy White House began to doubt the integrity of military reporting from Vietnam. "The civilians asked to have a set of cable machines in the White House so this sort of thing could be monitored, and the military readily agreed. The next day some fourteen machines were moved into the White House basement, grinding out millions of routine words per day, and the civilians knew that they were beaten by the sheer volume, that it was impossible to monitor it all. They surrendered and the machines were moved out, almost as quickly as they had been moved in." (*The Best and the Brightest* [Random House, 1972], pp. 271–72.) If HEW were to send to the Executive Office of the President all its correspondence with regional offices and with state and local grantees, that office would be similarly overwhelmed.

3. In practice, the new emphasis on management has been expressed in directions to the agencies to pursue "management by objectives." Systematic statements of objectives are supposed to clarify the rationale for budget decisions. If there is any change here, it is in the rhetoric that accompanies the budget process and in the division of labor within the OMB, not in the role of the President's staff. See *National Journal*, June 2, 1973, pp. 783–93; *National Journal Reports*, November 17, 1973, pp. 1703–09, and April 27, 1974, pp. 609–18; and *Science*, vol. 183 (January 25, 1974), pp. 286–90. For a more general analysis of the OMB's new management role, but with attention specifically to intergovernmental relations, see Gary Bombardier, "The Role of the Office of Management and Budget in Intergovernmental Relations" (manuscript, Brookings, 1973).